Oil & Tempera
PAINTING
500 *questions & answers*

Oil & Tempera
PAINTING

500 questions & answers

BY FREDERIC TAUBES

WATSON-GUPTILL PUBLICATIONS

CONTENTS

PART 1 OIL PAINTING MATERIALS—
Their Choice and Preparation

1 The Support: Canvas, Panel and
   Their Preparation   9
2 Composition Boards; Plywood; Wood
   Panels; Illustration Board   16
3 Brushes and Palette Knives   24
4 Glues and Other Adhesives   28
5 Oils   32
6 Solvents   39
7 Siccatives (Dryers)   43
8 Resins; Varnishes and Varnishing
   Paintings; Balsams; Painting Medium
   Formulas   45
9 Waxes   57
10 Miscellaneous Materials   59
11 Pigments and Oil Paints   61
12 Grinding Pigments by Hand   77
13 Simple Tests of Paints and Pigments   86
14 Old Masters' Pigments   92

PART 2 OIL PAINTING METHODS

15 Toned Ground; Underpainting;
   Imprimatura   101
16 Painting; Glazing; Scumbling   107
17 Cleaning; Repairing   114

PART 3 TEMPERA PAINTING

18 Egg-Tempera Painting   127
19 Oil-Tempera Painting   133
INDEX   139

PART 1

OIL PAINTING MATERIALS
Their Choice and Preparation

CHAPTER 1

The Support: Canvas, Panel and Their Preparation

1. *Q. Which support is most commonly used?*

A. Canvas. Dealers in artists' materials carry a variety of canvas fabrics (cotton, linen, etc.) in various forms: mounted on board to make "panels"; stretched on wooden frames; and by the yard from the roll, for the painter to stretch on stretchers made for the purpose.

2. *Q. Which of these forms of canvas is best?*

A. Much depends on the quality of the canvas itself. Most of the so-called canvas panels have nothing to recommend them—they are unsatisfactory. Canvas by the yard is usually the painter's first choice. It comes in a variety of weaves, some coarse, some fine.

3. *Q. Is linen canvas better than cotton?*

A. Not necessarily. The best cotton is superior to poor linen. However, linen of superior quality cannot be matched by any cotton material. Generally, for small sizes (up to about 20" x 24") cotton canvas can be very well used, however, the texture of the cotton fabric is, unless well covered with the underpainting, monotonous, hence quite unattractive.

4. *Q. What choice—prepared canvas or raw canvas?*

A. While some painters prepare their own canvas, as we shall see in a moment, many others select the prepared "commercial" canvas and proceed at once with their painting. Such canvas has been "sized" (Q. 12) and then coated with priming (Q. 22) to form the "ground" or working surface upon which the painting is done.

5. *Q. What type of ground does the commercial canvas carry? What are its constituents?*

A. An oil ground. In former years this usually consisted of white lead pigment mixed with a binder of linseed oil. Today the white pigments are generally titanium white, zinc oxide, and barium sulphate. (For a discussion of such pigments, *see* Ch. 11.) The binder is linseed oil in combination with a resin dissolved in a petrol distillate.

6. *Q. Is a ground prepared with white lead preferable to one made with other white pigments—titanium, zinc white, etc?*

A. In most respects a white lead ground is more desirable. (For the reasons *see* Q. 23.)

7. *Q. Why do some grounds yellow, while others remain comparatively white?*

A. White oil grounds tend to yellow, especially when kept in darkness (as in the case of rolled canvas, for example). The yellowing of oil grounds prepared with titanium white is much less pronounced.

8. *Q. Can a yellowed ground be bleached.*

A. Generally a few days of exposure to strong daylight in addition to a few hours of exposure to indirect sunlight will bleach a yellowed white lead oil ground.

9. *Q. Why is the ground or priming of most commercial canvases light gray in color?*

A. The manufacturer purposely colors it light gray because such a yellowing as will gradually take place will not be noticeable on a gray ground.

10. *Q. What are the advantages of a studio-prepared ground over one commercially prepared?*

A. The painter can control the character of his ground. Through the selection of a raw fabric suited to his purpose (which he stretches on a stretcher) and through his method of applying the ground, he is able to obtain any desired texture.

11. *Q. How does the painter prepare his own canvas?*

A. His first move is to coat the canvas with what is known as "size."

12. *Q. What is a "size," and what purpose does it serve?*

A solution of glue (or gelatin) and water. When applied, this size serves to isolate the fiber of the canvas from contact with oil paint, which otherwise would make the fabric brittle, eventually destroying it. (*See* Ch. 4.)

13. *Q. What kind of glue or gelatin is used?*

A. See Questions 97, 104.

14. *Q. What is the proportion of glue or gelatin and water in the size?*

A. One ounce of first-quality glue, or ¾ of an ounce of gelatin, should be dissolved in one pint of water.

15. *Q. Which is better, a liquid or a gelled size?*

A. A liquid size should not be used on canvas. When the size reaches room temperature it will congeal to a soft gel. As such it should be used on a canvas.

16. *Q. How should the gel be applied?*

A. First, using a large palette knife, crush the gel to a mush; then, with the same knife, spread it very thinly over the canvas.

17. *Q. Which is preferable, liquid or the jellified size?*

A. A jellified size applied with a palette knife will seal the openings in the fabric and thus prevent the priming from penetrating to the back of the canvas.

18. *Q. How would a too strong glue solution affect the canvas, and what are the disadvantages of a too weak size?*

A. The first will cause cracks on the canvas; the second will not isolate the fiber sufficiently—hence it will permit the oil to soak through.

19. *Q. Should the back of the canvas be sized, too?*

A. Not unless priming the back with oil paint is also contemplated.

20. *Q. How can one prevent the size from putrefying?*

A. To 1 pint of the size, add 1 to 1½ teaspoonfuls of a 10 per cent phenol solution (or keep the size in the refrigerator).

21. *Q. Should the canvas be smoothed with sandpaper before or after sizing?*

A. After sizing. Some canvases after sizing become excessively rough; therefore they should be sandpapered. The sandpapered surface should then be sized once more in order to protect the fiber of the canvas in case it has been deprived of its protective film.

OIL GROUND

22. *Q. Once the canvas has been sized, what is the next preparatory move.*

A. As soon as the glue or gelatin size is thoroughly dry (which, depending on room temperature and atmospheric moisture, may take from one to six hours), the canvas is ready for priming with white lead oil paint to form the painting ground.

23. *Q. Why is white lead preferable to titanium or zinc white for priming? (See also Q. 6, 7.)*

A. White lead is the traditional, time-tested material. It has been used for centuries and has proved to be absolutely permanent.

24. *Q. Should one use tube white lead for priming?*

A. It is suitable but more expensive than the commercial canned white lead.

25. *Q. What is the difference between canned white lead and tube white lead?*

A. The former yellows more because it is prepared with a cheaper grade of oil.

26. *Q. How can one improve the white color of the canned white lead?*

A. By mixing 3 or 4 ounces of titanium white with refined linseed oil to a soft paste, adding this paste to 1 pound of white lead paint, working the two materials together thoroughly.

27. *Q. When used for priming, what should be the consistency of the white lead paint?*

A. It should be sufficiently liquid to produce a thin layer on the canvas. Therefore, white lead of normal consistency should be thinned a little with Copal Painting Medium. (*See* Q. 212.)

28. *Q. How many layers of white priming should be applied to a canvas?*

A. On a fine fabric, one layer will be sufficient. On

rougher fabrics, two primings will be necessary or, in exceptional cases, three.

29. *Q. How soon should these primings follow one another?*

A. Allow twelve to twenty-four hours in between.

30. *Q. What instruments should be used for applying the oil priming to the canvas?*

A. Only the palette knife, because it makes the priming material sink into the interstices of the fabric, a thing which the brush will not do in like manner.

31. *Q. How long should one wait before painting on such a studio-prepared white lead ground?*

A. From one week to a month or more, depending on the thickness of the ground. The longer one waits, the better, especially when titanium white has been mixed with white lead; this is because the latter retards drying.

32. *Q. How can one accelerate the drying of an oil ground?*

A. By adding 2 drops of cobalt siccative to 1 ounce of white lead or by mixing the priming with some umber or manganese blue oil color.

GESSO GROUND (See also Ch. 2)

33. *Q. Is the oil ground priming the only one used?*

A. No. The "gesso" ground is also employed.

34. *Q. What is a "gesso" ground?*

A. A material such as whiting, gypsum, or titanium white bound by a size.

35. *Q. When should such a gesso ground be used?*

A. Only on panels (*see* Ch. 2).

36. Q. *Should gesso be applied when cold or warm?*

A. When the gesso solution prepared with glue or gelatin attains normal room temperature, it will jellify; in this condition it will not be brushable. Therefore, when working with the gesso it is advisable to keep the solution warm, in a double boiler. When casein is used instead of the glue, the size will not jellify.

37. Q. *How can one preserve the gesso solution from decomposing?*

A. Keep it in a refrigerator; or add to 1 pint of the gesso solution 1 to 1½ teaspoonfuls of a 10 per cent solution of phenol. Before using gesso which has been stored for some time, replace the water lost through evaporation.

38. Q. *What deficiencies will gesso possess which are too weak or too strong in glue content?*

A. In the first case the gesso will be too absorbent, hence it will draw the oil from the subsequent oil priming. When gesso contains too much glue, it will become too non-absorbent.

CHAPTER **2**

Composition Boards; Plywood;
Wood Panels; Illustration Board

39. *Q. Is a rigid support, such as a properly built panel of wood, preferable to an elastic support such as a canvas?*

A. From the viewpoint of permanence, an oil painting executed on a first-rate panel has a better chance of being well preserved than one executed on canvas. The paint film on a canvas support is subject to a certain type of crack which will not appear on a panel, because the paint film is practically immobilized on the latter (that is, providing that the panel itself does not deteriorate).

40. *Q. What other advantages does a first-rate panel support offer?*

A. All the damages so common to a canvas, such as scratches, abrasions, etc, are much more easily repaired when they appear on a panel. In other words, when a panel is used, the necessity for a professional restorer to mend or reline a damaged painting is largely eliminated.

41. *Q. What are the disadvantages of a rigid support?*

A. First, the canvas grain, which may sometimes be utilized effectively in painting, is not present on a panel; second, being rigid, the panel does not respond very well to a vigorous exercise of the brush; third, and very important, work with a palette knife is quite limited on a rigid surface. (*See also* Q. 53.)

42. *Q. When contemplating the use of a rigid support, which one is the most suitable under modern conditions?*

A. The first choice is the composition board known under the trade name of Masonite. Other supports which can be used are plywood; plywood covered with linen; solid wood panels; and, finally, a good illustration board or academy board.

43. *Q. What is Masonite?*

A. A composition board manufactured by the Masonite Corporation, consisting of wood fibers welded together under heat and extreme pressure. It comes in two grades: Tempered Masonite and Untempered Masonite.

44. *Q. What is the difference between the two products, and which is better suited to the painter's purpose?*

A. *Tempered Masonite* is obtained by subjecting the material to a special process which consists of impregnating the board with a tempering liquid and then polymerizing the liquid by baking. This increases the tensile and transverse strength, and resistance to abrasion; it also reduces moisture absorption. However, the painter should use the untempered kind, which is an all wood fiberboard made from cleaned, refined, exploded wood fiber, felted and pressed into board form in heated flatbed hydraulic presses. No chemical binders are added. It is grainless and knotless, has great resistance to moisture, no cross grain, and is far denser than wood. One side is smooth, the other having a screen impression surface with a canvas-like texture. The smooth side should be used for painting. (Q. 58.) It is said that a ground applied to the tempered Masonite may crack and yellow.

45. *Q. Should a Masonite panel be reinforced to prevent it from warping?*

A. Small sizes up to 16 by 20 inches need not be braced as they are not inclined to warp. It is advisable, however, to reinforce larger sizes—Masonite comes as large as 4 by 8 feet. If the picture frame which ultimately holds the panel is built firmly enough, it may serve very well as a bracing for the panel.

46. *Q. How thick should the Masonite panel be?*

A. One-eighth of an inch is the thickness usually recommended. It can also be obtained in thicknesses ranging up to 5/16 of an inch, but such panels are difficult to handle because of their weight.

47. *Q. What is plywood?*

A. A type of laminated wood made up of an odd number of veneer sheets glued together under pressure, the grains of the alternate layers usually being at right angles to one another. Some such boards are glued with waterproof adhesive.

48. *Q. How good is plywood panel as a support?*

A. Generally a well-glued-together plywood panel is more resistant to warping and cracking than are solid wooden boards.

49. *Q. Which is the best commercial plywood obtainable?*

A. A five-ply birch, 13/16 of an inch thick.

50. *Q. What kinds of wood were used by the old masters in the preparation of panels?*

A. Oak, linden, and pine were the most popular in northern countries. Birch, fir, and walnut were also used. The Italians preferred chestnut and poplar. Besides these, panels made from cedar, mahogany, olive, larch, cypress, and pear woods were not uncommon. These panels were solid, not veneered.

51. *Q. How should one prevent solid wood panels from warping?*

A. Cradling is the best method. A cradle consists of strips of wood glued to the panel (parallel to the grain of the panel), through which thinner strips are inserted in a lattice-like fashion through openings prepared for them before the heavy strips are glued on. These cross-strips are not glued but lie flat against the panel, thus being able to give, as the panel contracts or expands.

52. *Q. Is the use of wood panels recommended today?*

A. Under present-day conditions, wood panels are undesirable for the following reasons: An expertly prepared panel should be made of well-seasoned wood, which should be backed or cradled. Such a panel would be very expensive. Moreover, wood panels should be kept out of the range of steam heat as such heat may eventually destroy the best of them.

53. *Q. Why did the old masters often use wooden panels?*

A. The early tempera painters used panels because they suited their techniques. The oil painters of the early Renaissance employed panels chiefly because of traditional reasons. In the 16th Century, however, canvas was the customary choice.

54. *Q. What other rigid supports can be used for oil painting?*

A. Illustration board or "Academy" board. The first must be sized by the artist; the second is a millboard coated by the manufacturer with oil priming and obtainable ready for use from the artists' materials dealer.

55. *Q. How does one size an illustration board?*

A. Apply to it a weak size prepared from ¼-½ ounce of gelatin to 1 quart of water. Or, brush onto the board as many layers of fixative as needed to make it largely non-absorbent.

56. *Q. How permanent are these supports?*

A. Academy board is rather inferior. A rag-made illustration board, or a rag-made paper support is, however, permanent.

57. *Q. How can one impart greater durability to a plywood panel?*

A. By gluing fine-grained raw canvas to both sides. The canvas should previously be dipped into a size (glue, 3 ounces; water, 1 pint) and then placed on the board, moistened generously with the size. (The size should be kept hot in order to prevent congealing.) This method was often practiced by the old masters in connection with solid wood panels.

58. *Q. How should one prime a Masonite panel?*

A. Before priming the smooth side of the panel (the side marked by a wire screen is unsuitable for painting because of its ugly texture) it should be roughened somewhat with course sandpaper in order to insure better adhesion of the priming. In case the panel is not backed (Q. 45), both sides should be primed. The priming should consist of size (1½ to 2 ounces of glue to 1 pint of water) mixed with enough titanium white to a liquid of milky consistency. A thicker solution would leave brush marks which would influence adversely subsequent painting.

59. *Q. Why is titanium white preferable to the older materials used for gessoing, such as zinc white, whiting, etc.?*

A. The hiding power of titanium white is greatly superior to all other whites. Hence it can be used in much thinner solutions.

60. *Q. Why should white lead not be used for gessoing?*

A. It is toxic in aqueous solutions and, unless it is ground in oil, it may darken.

61. *Q. In what manner should the priming be done?*

A. Two coats applied crosswise with a large, preferably soft-hair brush will suffice. Allow the first coat to dry before brushing on the second priming.

62. *Q. Should the gesso solution be hot or cold when applied?*

A. A gesso priming with a relatively high glue content will congeal quickly in cool temperatures; therefore it should be kept in a hot-water bath. One should also consider the water evaporation from the priming solution, and replenish this loss during prolonged working periods.

63. *Q. Can one paint with oil colors on an absorbent gesso ground?*

A. Pure gesso ground is used principally for painting in egg-tempera and casein colors; that is, in instances where no oil, or very little oil, is used in the medium.

64. *Q. Should a gesso ground be sandpapered?*

A. It all depends on the painter's preference. If desired, a 00 sandpaper can be used for removing all undesirable texture or roughness.

65. *Q. How can one reduce the absorbency of the gesso ground?*

A. Any of the following methods can be used; however, the first appears to be the most suitable: (1) Apply gelatin or glue size on top of the gesso ground (to safeguard this ground against cracking, the size should not be stronger than that used in preparation of the gesso) ; or (2) coat the gesso with a shellac solution consisting of white shellac (best commercial grade) thinned with 2 to 4 parts of alcohol; or (3) cover the gesso with copal varnish. If needed, repeat the procedure after the first coat has solidified.

66. *Q. What other binder can be used for priming a panel?*

A. Instead of glue, casein can be used.

67. *Q. What is casein?*

A. An adhesive prepared from curd of milk and lime (Q. 107).

68. *Q. How can one prepare a casein solution suitable for gessoing?*

A. One ounce of dry casein should be soaked in 12 ounces of hot water for about an hour. Then 1 ounce of ammonia (26° Baumé ammonium hydroxide) is added under constant agitation. When the solution is complete, add enough titanium white to form a liquid of milky consistency and enough opacity to produce a white priming.

69. *Q. What are the advantages of casein gesso?*

A. The solution does not jellify; there is no need to keep it warm.

70. *Q. Should one use casein priming for oil painting?*

A. It is suitable for painting in oil, but the absorbency of the priming should be reduced. This is done by coating the priming with casein size (that is, casein-water solution without the gesso material).

71. *Q. Can one use casein priming on canvas?*

A. No. It is too brittle, and liable to crack on an elastic support.

72. *Q. How can one prevent the casein solution from decomposing?*

A. Add to 1 pint of the solution 1 to 1½ teaspoonfuls of a 10 per cent phenol solution.

OIL PRIMING

73. *Q. Can one prime a Masonite panel with oil paint, and how should one prepare the oil paint?*

A. White lead paint (flake white) should be thinned to a loose consistency with copal varnish so as not to leave any brush marks. (For copal varnish *see* Q. 187.)

74. *Q. In what manner should the oil be applied to a panel?*

A. The smooth side of the panel should be thinly covered with paint, and 12 to 24 hours later a second coat should be applied.

75. *Q. How long should one wait before painting on it?*

A. A thin ground can be overpainted in 1 to 2 weeks.

76. *Q. Which is preferable, a gesso or an oil ground?*

A. It is all a matter of personal choice.

CHAPTER 3

Brushes and Palette Knives

77. *Q. What kinds of brushes are used in oil painting?*

A. Bristle brushes, sable or fitch brushes, and soft-hair blenders.

78. *Q. What are the properties and characteristics of the bristle brush?*

A. Bristle brushes are made of hogs' hair. The so-called "brights" are made with short bristles, and the "flats" with longer hairs. Generally, the best quality brushes are made of hair which curves from both ends of the ferrule toward the middle; the hairs placed in the middle are straight. The hairs in cheaper brushes form a mass which is usually narrow at the ferrule and wider at the end. Also, the expensive brushes have firmer and more elastic hair than the cheaper ones.

79. *Q. What kinds of sable (or fitch) brushes should be used, and what purposes do they serve?*

A. The best quality is made of red sable, which is the tail hair of the kolinsky. (Several species of Asiatic mink are known as kolinsky.) Fitch brushes (so-called Russian sable) are good substitutes for the red sable brushes. Where a soft brush stroke or a delicate blending of colors is desired, a sable brush is indispensable. Sables are made in flat and round shapes. Large flat brushes, an inch or more in size, come with short handles, indicating that they are used chiefly in watercolor. However, they are also valuable in certain oil techniques for blending.

80. *Q. What is a soft-hair blender?*

A. A soft-hair brush made from a variety of hairs, mostly squirrel; it is better suited to delicate blending than a sable brush because the very soft hair does not have the power to agitate a paint film. These blenders may be had in a variety of shapes, but the most suitable are flat brushes ¾ to 1 inch wide.

81. *Q. What brushes should be used for varnishing?*

A. Practically any brush having elastic hair, but the utility brush, made of black bristle, is especially suitable. (To make it more elastic, it is advisable to reduce its thickness by cutting some of the bristles at the ferrule.) For small paintings, a brush 1 inch wide is practical; for large paintings, 1½ to 2 inches will be more appropriate. When a painting has not sufficiently hardened, the use of a harsh brush, such as one made of bristle, should be avoided, as it might injure a relatively soft painting. On a paint layer which has not dried throughout, a soft brush made of sable hair should be used.

82. *Q. What brush should be chosen for gessoing a canvas or a panel?*

A. The same brush as for varnishing—a utility brush 2 to 4 inches wide (depending on the size of the canvas).

83. *Q. Should a fuzzy brush be trimmed?*

A. No. Only the natural tips of the hairs are suitable in painting. These outer ends are called "flag" or "split ends."

84. *Q. How can one lengthen brushes which have been worn short?*

A. A French-made brush with hairs worn short can be made longer by heating the ferrule with a match and pulling the hairs part way out; sometimes their length can be increased by almost half an inch. American- and English-made brushes are set in a plastic which, unlike the pitch in which the French product is set, does not yield to heat. However, if one of these brushes is badly worn it can be made usable again by cutting off a little of the flattened part of the ferrule with a sharp-edged file. The hairs uncovered by this procedure are usually clogged with paint or plastic which must be softened with a paint remover.

85. *Q. How can one reshape the hair of a brush which has become bent or otherwise ruffled through improper storage?*

A. Moisten the hair with mucilage or gelatin, press it to correct shape, and let it remain for a few days. Then wash it out. If the hairs are badly twisted, bind a thread around the bristles in addition to the adhesive to secure their proper position. Brushes should dry with the hairs pointed downward.

86. *Q. What is the best method of cleaning a brush still moist with oil paint?*

A. To remove the surplus of wet paint, first squeeze the brush with a newspaper; then wash the brush with soap and warm water.

87. *Q. How should one remove dried paint from a brush?*

A. Soak the brush for a short time in benzene, xylene, or a paint remover; then wash it thoroughly with soap and warm water.

88. *Q. How should one clean moist or hardened resin from a brush?*

A. The brush should first be rinsed in mineral spirits or in any of the paint thinners (benzene, xylene, etc., Q. 138) and then washed in soap and water.

89. *Q. What type of palette knife is useful in painting?*

A. One having a straight, flexible blade. A blade which is trowel-shaped or has no "give" is unsuitable.

90. *Q. What type of palette knife should be used for underpainting? (For underpainting, see Ch. 15.)*

91. *Q. What palette knife is most convenient for mixing pigment with oil?*

A. A stiff knife; also the trowel-shaped variety. The wider the blade, the more easily the paint can be manipulated.

92. *Q. What knife is best for scraping dry paint from the palette?*

A. A putty knife.

93. *Q. How should one dull the blade of a knife which has become too sharp through much use?*

A. Hold the blade at right angles to a sheet of fine emery paper and rotate the knife vigorously. The burr which will form along the edge of the blade during such manipulation should be removed with the emery paper.

94. *Q. What kind of palette should the painter use?*
A. This is a matter of personal preference. Some painters prefer a palette made of wood; others choose enamel or plastic palettes. A palette about 20 inches square, of wood, seems the most suitable. A wooden palette should first be primed with linseed oil to make it non-absorbent. Eventually, it attains a neutral color which is most agreeable, whereas the white color of a synthetic palette forever exerts a disturbing influence on the eyes.

CHAPTER 4

Glues and Other Adhesives

95. *Q. What kind of adhesives are used by the painter, and what purpose do they serve?*

A. Glue, gelatin, casein, gum arabic. The first three are used to size a canvas or a panel before priming. Gum arabic (gum senegal) is used in the preparation of water-colors and tempera paint; *see* definitions, Question 108.

96. *Q. Of what is glue made?*

A. Animal matter, such as hides, claws, hoofs, mucous membranes, bones.

97. *Q. Which is considered the best quality of glue?*

A. Glue made of hide or rabbit-skin clippings. The first is known as "hide" glue; the second as "rabbit-skin" glue. American rabbit-skin glue is said to be as good as the well-known French product. Formerly, the German Cologne glue made of hide clippings enjoyed great reputation. It is best for the painter to buy American rabbit-skin glue and thus become accustomed to using a uniform quality of the material.

98. *Q. What are the chief characteristics of a good glue?*

A. Great adhesive power; absence of impurities, free acid, and fat; capacity to jellify at normal room temperature in a weak solution such as 1 ounce of glue to 1 pint of water.

99. *Q. How can one recognize good glue before dissolving it?*

A. When the glue is obtained in sheets, one should test the sheets for color and brittleness. A superior glue is of light brown color and is translucent. A dark brown, or muddy, blackish appearance of the glue (with the exception of rabbit-skin glue, which is of dark color) will indicate that the material has been burned or otherwise improperly prepared. When a glue sheet can be broken easily with one's hands, the glue is inferior. The resilience of good sheet glue is such that, especially in smaller pieces, it can be broken only with a hammer, but hardly with one's fingers. A glue of inferior quality will also fail to jellify at normal room temperatures, even in relatively high concentrates such as 2 ounces of glue to 1 pint of water. Inferior glue will not only lack sufficient adhesive power, but later it will also invite mildew and mold.

In addition to the sheet glue, glue is also sold in the form of flakes or pearls, or ground to dust. The reliability of such glues is uneven and varies with different manufacturers.

100. *Q. What kinds of glue should be avoided?*

A. Bone glue, which, as its name implies, is made from bones; fish glue, usually sold in liquid form.

101. *Q. How should one dissolve glue?*

A. It should be soaked overnight in water (cold or hot), and then melted in hot water. Prolonged boiling of glue reduces its adhesive power.

102. *Q. How can one prevent a glue solution from decomposing?*

A. Keep in a refrigerator, or add to it 1 per cent of a 10 per cent phenol solution.

GELATIN

103. *Q. What is gelatin?*

A. Gelatin is the purest form of glue. It comes in very thin transparent sheets, flakes, or in granulated form.

104. *Q. What kind of gelatin can be obtained?*

A. There is a technical grade which should be used by the painter. A highly refined gelatin is used in cooking; it is not very suitable for sizing, but it can be used in an emergency.

105. *Q. Is gelatin preferable to other types of glue?*

A. Gelatin jellifies more rapidly. Also, when speedy dissolving of the adhesive is required, gelatin is preferable to glue because it dissolves quickly in hot water.

106. *Q. How can one prevent a gelatin solution from de-composing?*

A. Add to 1 pint of the solution 1 per cent of a 10 per cent phenol solution, or keep in the refrigerator.

CASEIN

107. *Q. What is casein?*

A. As we have seen (Q. 67), casein is an adhesive prepared from curd of milk and lime. (The formulation of casein varies with different manufacturers.) This adhesive is one of the oldest known, and is especially suitable for use on panels and frames in connection with gesso (Q. 69); it may also serve as a substitute for glue for carpentering purposes, particularly where greater resistance to moisture is desired. In contrast with glue, which remains hygroscopic after it has dried, casein, upon drying, becomes partially water insoluble. It is also more suitable than glue for the preparation of casein tempera colors and casein emulsions (*see* Tempera Painting, Ch. 18; for preparation of casein size and gesso, *see* Q. 68).

GUM ARABIC

108. *Q. What is gum arabic and what purpose does it serve?*

A. It is an exudate of several species of the acacia tree which grows in Africa, India, and Australia. It comes in small, yellowish, opalescent lumps. In order to dissolve gum arabic in water, it should first be reduced to powder and then slowly stirred into boiling water, in the proportion of 1 part of the gum to 2 parts of water. Boiling should be discontinued as soon as the gum is placed in the water. In this form, gum arabic will serve in the preparation of watercolors and tempera emulsions. In weak solution, gum arabic can also be used for sizing paper.

109. *Q. How can gum arabic be preserved?*

A. To prevent it from mildewing, a piece of camphor should be placed in the bottle containing the solution. Also, a 1 per cent addition of a 10 per cent phenol solution can be employed for this purpose. In preparation of watercolors, use powdered U.S.P. quality of gum arabic.

CHAPTER 5

Oils

110. *Q. What oils are used in painting?*

A. Chiefly linseed oil; also a poppy-seed oil and walnut oil (Q. 137).

111. *Q. What is cold-pressed linseed oil?*

A. An oil which is obtained by pressing the seeds of the plant which produces linen fiber. To be suitable for painting, the raw oil must be freed from impurities which it contains, such as albuminoid and mucilaginous matter. Cold-pressed oil is generally not obtainable today in the U.S. Oil labeled as "cold-pressed" is, as a rule, a refined type of steam-extracted oil.

112. *Q. How is steam-extracted oil refined?*

A. There are two methods of refining the oil: (1) acid refining; (2) alkali refining. In the first, acid is used to remove mucilaginous matter. After filtering and washing the oil appears pale in color and its acid number is usually high (Q. 121). Such an oil is unsuitable for heat-processing and it is used chiefly for industrial—not for artistic—purposes. The alkali-refined oil is purified with small quantities of concentrated alkali. This removes the impurities and excess free acid and sweetens the oil (*see* Q. 123). The oil is then thoroughly washed and goes through a number of cycles of "winterizing" (chilling) and filtering. The end product is very light, pure, and neutral. This type of oil is used generally in the U.S. by the artists. The alkali process does not cause deterioration of the oil, and the soaps that are produced in the treatment are so thoroughly washed out that no traces of them can be found. This oil is also used for the manufacture of standoil.

113. *Q. What are the advantages of linseed oil?*

A. Because of the chemical composition of linseed oil, its durability and drying properties are superior to all other drying oils. These properties are due to the presence of glycerides of linoleic and linolenic acids, which form the tough skin of the dried oil known as linoxyn.

114. *Q. What is the disadvantage of linseed oil?*

A. Its tendency to yellow.

115. *Q. What causes linseed oil to yellow, and what circumstances contribute to its yellowing?*

A. The yellowing is due to the presence of (a) the glycerides of the linoleic acids and (b) impurities such as chlorophyll (the latter is almost entirely eliminated by the refining process). Yellowing of oil is accelerated by exposure of the drying paint film to moisture and darkness. (A dry oil film will also suffer in the presence of moisture and darkness.)

116. *Q. Should one use the kind of linseed oil commonly sold in hardware and paint stores?*

A. No. The industrial linseed oil is not suitable for permanent painting. It will cause the colors to yellow and to darken.

117. *Q. What is meant by the terms "wetting power" and "leveling" of oil?*

A. "Wetting power" is the capacity to wet or bind thoroughly each particle of pigment. "Leveling" implies that the paint takes on a characteristic of enamel paint; that is, it levels off without leaving brush marks. Such paint is generally not suitable for pastose painting. (*See* Q. 131.)

118. *Q. What is a "short" paint?*

A. A paint which is stiff and crisp, and which, when piled up, retains its original shape or "configuration," as it is known.

119. *Q. What is a "long" paint?*

A. A paint which levels off.

ACIDITY AND POLYMERIZATION OF OIL

120. *Q. What is neutral linseed oil, and what are its characteristics?*

A. Oil which has no free acid, or oil possessing an acid number up to 2, which is considered low. Such an oil has little wetting power and it produces, with most of the pigments, a short, stiff paste.

121. *Q. How does free acid develop in oil, and in what manner does it influence the paint?*

A. While in the process of drying, through oxidation and heating, the oil becomes polymerized and develops free acid. This means that oil which has been heated or exposed to air will develop free acid and will become viscous. Such an oil is sun-thickened oil (Q. 125), standoil (Q. 130), and blown oil (Q. 134). Also, through long storage, even a neutral oil will change its acid value. The acid value influences the consistency of paint. The higher the acid value, the greater the wetting and leveling capacity of the oil, and the longer and stringier will be the body of the paint. The acid value of oil should be carefully considered before grinding pigments.

122. *Q. How does one recognize the presence of free acid?*

A. The simplest way is to smell the oil. Sour odor will indicate the presence of free acid; a neutral oil will have a sweet odor. Also, blue litmus paper (obtainable at the drug store) will turn red when dipped into an oil of acid content.

123. *Q. How can one eliminate free acid from the oil?*

A. Put into 1 pint of oil 1 teaspoonful of calcium oxide (quick lime) and heat the oil; shake mixture and let it settle. Calcium oxide should be allowed to remain at the bottom of the bottle; it absorbs acid formation during the storage of oil. Bottles should always be filled to the top and well stopped to prevent access of air.

124. *Q. What is polymerized oil?*

A. When oil is exposed to the sun or to artificial heat (or is allowed to age) certain changes in molecular structure of the oil take place. These changes are known as polymerization. There are various stages of polymerization, depending upon the length of time the oil is exposed to heat (or air). Oil which has been polymerized under a tight vacuum gains greater wetting power, becomes viscous, and is not inclined to yellow. When used for grinding pigments it will react like oil which possesses free acid, that is, it will produce a "long" paint. (Q. 119, 130)

125. *Q. What is sun-thickened oil?*

A. When oil is exposed to the action of sun rays during a period of 4 to 8 weeks it becomes polymerized and thickens to the consistency of honey.

126. *Q. Why is sun-thickened oil considered a more desirable painting medium than the ordinary oil?*

A. Sun-thickened oil is viscous, polymerized, and possesses greater wetting power. Its durability will also be increased and its drying qualities and color improved. Moreover, such an oil will impart greater gloss to the paint with which it is mixed, and, because of its greater leveling property, will blend the colors more effectively.

127. *Q. Can one use straight sun-thickened linseed oil as a painting medium?*

A. If its viscosity is not excessive, it can be used undiluted; otherwise, an admixture of varnish or turpentine will be needed (*see* page 55, Painting Medium Formulas).

128. *Q. Should linseed oil be placed in leaden vessels during the time of its exposure to sun?*

A. It is said that this procedure accelerates the drying of oil, but I could not verify this. However, the lead seems to be instrumental in effecting the elimination of certain impurities from the oil. When exposed in a glass or tin vessel, the oil will yield much less sediment.

129. *Q. How should one treat the oil during the time of exposure?*

A. The vessel should be covered with a glass plate in order to prevent access of dirt, and the surface of the oil should be slightly agitated once a day to prevent the forming of a skin. One should be careful not to agitate the sediment or it will mix again with the oil.

130. *Q. What is standoil?*

A. A linseed oil which has been heated to around 600°F. for a period of hours under a vacuum or under carbon dioxide—in other words, in the absence of oxygen.

131. *Q. What are the characteristics of standoil?*

A. This oil is considered to be the best of all oils used for painting because it is not inclined to yellow, and because its resistance to moisture and atmospheric attacks is greater than that of any other form of linseed oil. It dries to an exceedingly tough film; but since it is not exposed to oxidation during the process of thickening, it does not dry as quickly as sun-thickened oil. It has strong leveling and wetting properties, and imparts a high gloss to the paint with which it is mixed.

132. *Q. Is standoil, as sold on the market, of uniform quality?*

A. No. It is produced in various degrees of viscosity and its acid number may vary considerably. The highly polymerized linseed oil (known as heavy-body standoil) is not, because of its viscosity, very well suited for painting purposes; or at least, its usability is limited, unless it is diluted with a varnish or turpentine. Light-body standoil can be used undiluted for painting.

133. *Q. What is the characteristic property of all heat-processed oils when used as painting media?*

A. They promote fusion of paints.

134. *Q. What is blown oil?*

A. Linseed oil which has been exposed to air while processed by heat. Such oil possesses extreme viscosity and since it becomes partially oxidized by the air blown through it during the heating process, it dries rapidly and with extreme gloss. But it yellows and wrinkles considerably.

VARIOUS DRYING OILS

135. *Q. What advantages does poppy-seed oil offer?*

A. Its only advantage is its slow-drying property— that is, when one desires a slow-drying paint. However, this quality of poppy oil is not always present; it is also more or less offset when it is mixed with quick-drying pigments such as white lead, umber, prussian blue, etc. Therefore, to make the poppy oil effective, it should be mixed only with pigments which by nature dry slowly. Poppy oil yellows less than linseed oil; in all other characteristics, especially with respect to durability, it is inferior to linseed oil.

136. *Q. What are the uses of walnut oil?*

A. Like poppy oil, it does not possess the durability of linseed oil or its all-around good qualities. According to accounts, sun-thickened nut oil (as well as sun-thickened poppy oil) was widely used by some old masters, especially in Northern Italy. Walnut oil, like poppy oil, becomes rancid with age.

137. *Q. What other oils are used in preparation of paints?*

A. In industrial paints, china wood oil (tung oil), when polymerized, is quite important because of its great resistance to moisture. It is, however, unsuitable for artists' purposes because it dries slowly (in dry air), wrinkles easily, and yellows badly. In moist air it dries quickly, but this is not a true drying (through oxidation)—it simply coagulates because of colloidal changes. (The nut which yields the oil comes from China and the neighboring countries; it has been transplanted also to Florida and the lower Mississippi.) Soya bean oil is a slow-drying oil which forms a weak film; the semi-drying cottonseed oil has similar qualities. Both are used for preparation of industrial paints. The non-drying fish oil, which can be made drying by heating with siccatives, sometimes serves as an adulterant for paint-grinding mediums. Oil of cloves, produced from the blossoms (or branches) of the clove tree, can be used by the painter (in small addition, such as 1 to 5 per cent) to retard drying of oil paints. For best results, oil of cloves should be mixed with the painting medium as well as with the tube paints.

CHAPTER 6

Solvents

138. *Q. What solvents or thinners are commonly used by the painter?*

A. Turpentine, mineral spirits, benzene, xylene, acetone, kerosene, alcohol, and ammonia.

139. *Q. Which of these is the most common?*

A. Turpentine.

140. *Q. From what is turpentine derived?*

A. The best turpentine is distilled from the sap of pine; or by steam, from the pine wood which grows chiefly in Georgia and the Carolinas.

141. *Q. Under what trade name does best quality turpentine appear on the market?*

A. "Pure gum spirits of turpentine," "oil of turpentine," or "steam-distilled turpentine."

142. *Q. What is rosin or colophony?*

A. The resin (Ch. 8) left after the distillation of turpentine is commonly referred to as rosin or colophony.

143. *Q. Is the "pure gum spirits of turpentine," when fresh, entirely free from rosin?*

A. It still contains about 2 per cent rosin which, however, is unobjectionable. By redistillation, it can be entirely freed of it.

144. *Q. Can turpentine be stored for any length of time?*

A. Turpentine absorbs oxygen, produces rosin, and thickens with age; unless redistilled, aged turpentine is not suitable for use as a thinner. Bottles containing turpentine should be well filled and stopped to prevent oxidation.

145. *Q. What is steam-distilled turpentine?*

A. A turpentine, produced by the distillation of pine wood. Steam-distilled turpentine has greater solving strength than gum turpentine, but otherwise they differ little. Wood turpentine, a by-product of papermaking, and produced by destructive distillation of pine wood, should be avoided.

146. *Q. How does one recognize a good turpentine?*

A. Fresh turpentine should evaporate without leaving any residuum. Tests may be made on a glass plate. When spread on a filter paper, turpentine should leave no appreciable stain after evaporation. Old turpentine is less limpid than the fresh product, its smell is more aromatic, and its drying properties are deficient.

147. *Q. What solvent can be substituted for turpentine?*

A. Mineral spirits (sold commercially under the names Varnolene, Texaco Spirits, Sunoco Spirits) is a petroleum distillate which has similar properties to turpentine in its evaporation rate, miscibility with oils, and action on resins. However, turpentine has more "bite" on oil films than mineral spirits.

148. *Q. What advantages have mineral spirits over turpentine?*

A. They do not polymerize and, unlike turpentine, do not form any substances such as rosin.

149. *Q. What other petroleum solvents are produced today?*

A. V.M.&P. naphtha, a coal tar product much more volatile than mineral spirits, is chiefly used as a thinner for house paints. A still more powerful solvent is benzene, obtained by destructive distillation of coal tar; when fractioned, it yields the product known as benzol. (Benzol contains about two-thirds benzene and one-third toluene.) Toluene and xylene, both coal tar distillates, are the safest materials to use for dissolving dry paint and for softening paint and resin-hardened brushes. (Safe because the vapor is not deleterious.) Acetone is a still more powerful oil and resin solvent, used chiefly in prepartion of commercial paint removers.

150. *Q. For what is kerosene used?*

A. Because it evaporates very slowly, kerosene is suitable for loosening wet paint from grinding implements such as the ground glass plate, muller, etc. Once the paint which clings stubbornly to such surfaces is softened by kerosene, it can easily be washed away with soap and water.

151. *Q. What is anhydrous alcohol?*

A. A pure alcohol which contains no water. Such an alcohol is miscible with turpentine and the coal tar derivatives. Methyl alcohol (wood alcohol, shellac solvent) is also a powerful paint remover, sometimes used by restorers to remove aged varnish and paint films. Fixative is prepared with this type of alcohol.

152. *Q. For what is ammonia used?*

A. Because of its strong alkaline properties, diluted ammonia serves to cut thin films of oil and grease from the surface of paintings or oil grounds (*see* Q. 388). For cleaning old paintings concentrated ammonia — 28° Baumé — should be thinned with 3 to 5 parts of water.

153. *Q. What solvents should a painter use for cutting resin?*

A. Resins can be dissolved in turpentine or mineral spirits, also in petrol and coal tar derivatives. Some resins, like mastic, for example, are also soluble (or partially soluble) in alcohol.

154. *Q. What solvents are suitable for thinning oil?*

A. Turpentine or mineral spirits.

155. *Q. What solvents will clean paintings?*

A. Depending on the age and nature of the varnish film: Mineral spirits, benzene, xylene, acetone, saponine (for saponine *see* Q. 423).

156. *Q. Should the painter use commercial paint removers?*

A. No, because they contain paraffin (which prevents the solvents from rapid evaporation). Paraffin cannot easily be removed from the interstices and crevices of the paint. Moreover, these solvents are too powerful, hence their action on a paint film cannot be very well controlled.

CHAPTER 7

Siccatives (Dryers)

157. *Q. What is a siccative?*

A. A metallic salt, such as salt of lead, cobalt, or manganese, dissolved by heating in an oil or a volatile medium for the purpose of accelerating drying and oxidation of oils.

158. *Q. Which is the safest of all the siccatives?*

A. A dryer prepared from the salt of cobalt cooked in linseed oil or naphtha. The first is known as cobalt linoleate; and the second as cobalt naphthanate.

159. *Q. In what manner does a dryer affect the paint?*

A. Dryers promote absorption of oxygen by the paint film. Some (such as lead siccative) act through the mass of the paint, and are known as body dryers; others accelerate the drying of the top surface of the film and are called top dryers. Cobalt and manganese siccative belong to the latter category.

160. *Q. Is it advisable to add siccative to a thickly applied paint?*

A. No, because a tough skin forms quickly on a paint mixed with siccative and prevents the air from reaching the underlying layers. Thus the paint within will remain wet longer than it would without the siccative. On the other hand, thin applications dry quickly throughout.

161. *Q. How soon will paint dry when siccative is added?*

A. Depending upon climate, atmospheric moisture, and the characteristic of the pigment, thin paint will dry in 4 to 8 hours.

162. *Q. How much siccative should be added to the paint?*

A. An addition of about 1/10 to 1/5 of 1 per cent of cobalt siccative to the paint and to the medium is considered a safe proportion. That is, the paint and the painting medium should receive separately an addition of siccative. One may thus add to about 2 linear inches of the paint, as it comes from the tube, 1 drop of siccative, and to a tablespoonful of the medium, 1 drop of siccative.

163. *Q. What damages may be caused by an excess of siccative?*

A. Yellowing, darkening, and embrittlement of a paint film are the usual results from excessive use of siccative, because the metal will remain in the body of the paint, forever absorbing and releasing oxygen.

164. *Q. What other siccatives are on the market?*

A. Siccatif de Haarlem, a mild dryer of little value, and the more powerful Siccatif de Courtrai, which contains lead and manganese resinates. They are inferior to cobalt siccative.

165. *Q. How can one accelerate the drying of paint in case siccative is not at hand?*

A. Even a small addition of umber or manganese blue oil color (or dry pigment) will, through its siccative action, accelerate the drying of paint in a manner similar to a liquid dryer. (Umber contains manganese dioxide, which in itself is a powerful dryer.)

CHAPTER 8

Resins; Varnishes & Varnishing Paintings; Balsams; Painting Medium Formulas

166. *Q. What is a varnish?*

A. In common parlance, a solution of a resin in a volatile medium.

167. *Q. What is a resin, and which resins are used by the painter?*

A. Resins are exudates from coniferous trees; the following resins are used for varnishing and as constituents of painting media: damar, mastic and copal.

168. *Q. Where do these resins come from?*

A. Damar is found in the Malayas and in the Dutch East Indies. Mastic, an exudate of the pistachio tree, comes from the Islands of Chios in the Aegean Sea, and the chief source of copal is the Belgian Congo, hence the name, Congo copal.

169. *Q. What is a gum?*

A. In popular use the term gum refers to a resin in its natural state. Technically, however, gums are water-soluble exudates of trees.

170. *Q. Which are the soft and which are the hard resins, and how do they differ one from another?*

A. Damar and mastic are referred to as soft, and copal is a hard or fossil resin. The latter comes from trees now extinct, hence they are found underground, whereas the soft resins are obtained by tapping living trees. The

45

methods of preparation and the nature of the varnishes made from these resins are quite dissimilar. The soft resins are soluble in turpentine and all the volatile petroleum solvents, without any previous processing. The hard resins, on the other hand, must first be thermally processed (Q. 175) in order to make them soluble in turpentine and petroleum solvents. The films obtained from a hard resin are more durable and more resistant to atmospheric attacks than those produced from the soft resin. The chief difference between these resins, however, lies in the fact that both damar and mastic varnishes dry through evaporation of the solvent, which leaves the resin fused but otherwise unchanged, while the hard resin, on the other hand, partially polymerizes. It follows that in time copal will not disintegrate as easily as will damar or mastic.

171. *Q. Which is the most commonly used resin for varnishing and painting purposes?*

A. Damar; it is preferred to mastic because it possesses greater elasticity, retains a lighter color, and does not induce bloom (Q. 205).

172. *Q. What qualities of damar are on the market?*

A. The best quality is known as Singapore No. 1 (or Batavia No. 1). It comes in rather large, hazlenut-like lumps, and produces an almost colorless varnish. Singapore No. 2 comes in smaller chips which are sometimes discolored because of impurities embedded in the resin. Damar "seeds," so-called because this gum consists of tiny particles, are a still lower grade of gum. The hardness of the material may also differ, depending on its source of origin.

173. *Q. What grades of Congo copal are on the market?*

A. Among the many grades of copal used for various purposes, "water-white transparent" Congo copal and the "goose-flesh" Zanzibar copal have superior qualities. The first, because of its lower melting point, produces a lighter varnish.

174. *Q. How does one dissolve a soft resin in a volatile medium?* (For resin mediums *see* Ch. 6.)

A. The resin should be reduced to powder and placed in a bag made of several layers of cheesecloth, and submerged in a jar containing turpentine or mineral spirits. The bag serves as a filter and prevents foreign matter and impurities from passing into the medium. Damar will dissolve in the solvent within a day or two; mastic will need at least a week.

One may also melt the resins and then add the solvent. Damar becomes soft at 155°F. to 175°F. and melts at 210°F. to 235°F. Mastic softens at 130°F. and melts at 170°F. The solvent should be added to the melted resin in small quantities to prevent its congealing. However, if the solvent is heated, all of it can be added at one time. The only advantage of the melting process is that varnish may be obtained instantaneously by this means.

175. *Q. How can the hard resin be dissolved?*

A. As stated under Question 170, before a hard resin yields to a solvent such as turpentine or mineral spirits, it must be thermally processed; that is, it must be melted down. This is done by placing the resin (which should be first reduced to powder) in a vessel made of stainless steel or aluminum. (Iron or copper would affect adversely the color of the resin.) The resin is now subjected to a temperature of from 580°F. to 630°F., depending on its quality. After one hour's exposure to this heat the resin liquifies; when it starts to drip off the stirring paddle like hot oil, but before all the lumps disappear, the melt is poured through a strainer into shallow tin pans where it is allowed to solidify. It is then broken up into small pieces. In this state the resin is known as "run" resin; hence we refer to a run copal.

176. *Q. Is copal in the natural state soluble in any of the existing solvents?*

A. No. It is only partially soluble in butyl alcohol and tetrachlorethane, in which it forms a gel.

177. *Q. How can one combine copal and an oil medium?*

A. Reduce run copal to powder and add it gradually to the oil, which must be pre-heated to a temperature of 400°F. to 450°F. For this purpose, heat-treated oil such as standoil is preferable to linseed oil after a heating period of from 5 to 15 minutes, and will combine with the oil into a homogeneous solution. In order to ascertain whether the resin has been sufficiently incorporated with the oil, after about 10 minutes of heating, a few drops of the solution should be taken out, placed on a glass plate and permitted to cool. Upon cooling, if the mixture remains clear, a state of homogeneity has been reached; if, however, the mixture is cloudy, heating should be resumed. Upon finishing the heating process, the resin-oil mixture (copal or damar) should be filtered through a fine cloth while the compound is hot and still liquid. When cool, it becomes too viscous to be freed from any impurities it may contain.

178. *Q. Is it true that a hard resin varnish may cause cracking and discoloration on a painting?*

A. A properly prepared copal varnish is more durable than a soft resin varnish; it will not yellow more than the former nor will it cause a paint film to crack.

179. *Q. Are all commercial varnishes uniform in composition?*

A. No. Varnishes, especially those prepared from copal, vary as to quality and concentration of the resin, and composition of the solvents. (When speaking of copal varnish, I refer specifically to my own formulation as manufactured by Permanent Pigments of Cincinnati, Ohio, which differs radically from other formulations.) The dark colors of all the copal varnishes are, however, entirely unobjectionable.

180. *Q. Why are some damar varnishes cloudy and some clear?*

A. A suspension of damar wax (for waxes *see* Ch. 9) in the solution causes the cloudy appearance of the varnish. The presence of this wax does not impair the quality of the varnish. A small addition of anhydrous alcohol will dissolve the wax suspended in the varnish and clarify the solution—this may be agreeable to the eye, but does not improve the quality of the varnish.

181. *Q. What types of damar varnishes are sold, and how do they differ as to composition?*

A. There are three types of damar varnishes: retouching varnish, final picture varnish, and a heavy varnish solution for use in tempera emulsions. The differences are in the resin concentration. Also, the nature of the solvents may differ. Retouching varnish is generally made of 1 part of resin to 4 or 5 parts of the solvent. The picture varnish is usually a concentration of 1 to 3, and the heavy solution contains 1 part of resin to 1 or 2 parts of the solvent. (The first by weight, the second by liquid ounces.)

182. *Q. What purposes does retouching varnish serve?*

A. To bring out sunk-in colors on a fresh paint film.

183. *Q. What purposes does damar picture varnish serve?*

A. It is used as a final varnish on paintings one year old or older in order to bring out the true colors of the paint, to prevent dirt from becoming ingrained in the paint film, and to protect the paint film from atmosphere attacks.

184. *Q. What are the uses of copal varnish?*

A. (1) For thinning white lead in priming a panel (*see* Q. 73). (2) For varnishing well-dried paintings (at least 2 years old). (3) For imprimaturas (*see* Q. 358).

185. *Q. What are the uses of a resin-oil solution (Copal Concentrate)?*

A. Copal resins dissolved in oil instead of in a volatile medium (such as turpentine or mineral spirits) produce extremely viscous solutions. If one wishes to use a resin-oil color, a few drops of the copal-oil compound should be added to about 1 linear inch of the paint as it comes from the tube. (For Copal Concentrate, *see* Q. 212.)

186. *Q. Does varnish kept in a bottle remain in good condition indefinitely?*

A. Not necessarily. A varnish which is compounded in turpentine undergoes deterioration due to polymerization and oxidation of the turpentine (Q. 144). However, when dissolved in a petrol derivative, the quality of the varnish remains stable. When prolonged storage is contemplated, the turpentine varnish should be kept in well-filled and stoppered bottles, so as to inhibit rosin and acid formation.

187. *Q. How long does it take varnish to dry?*

A. The drying depends on the quality of the resin, the degree of the resin concentration, and the nature of the solvent. Damar resin of high quality, dissolved in fresh turpentine or mineral spirits, dries superficially in a few minutes. The solidification of the resin film continues for some time. Copal varnish solidifies more quickly and forms a more durable film.

188. *Q. Why do some paintings remain tacky for a long time after varnishing?*

A. Several factors may account for it: (1) an inferior resin; (2) old turpentine; (3) the presence of oil in varnish (some picture varnishes contain an addition of oil) ; (4) tackiness of the paint film itself. Such a paint surface will feel tacky, no matter how dry a varnish on top of it may be.

189. *Q. How soon should a painting be varnished?*

A. Retouching varnish can be applied on a painting at any time after it has dried superficially; that is, in one day or more, but the varnish does not last on a superficially dry painting.

190. *Q. Is it detrimental to a painting to varnish it before it is at least one year old?*

A. No. A coat of varnish will not harm a painting: it is too weak to cause cracking of the paint film. However, if glazes were used, it is safer to delay varnishing to permit their incorporation with the paint film rather than with the varnish.

191. *Q. Why should one delay the application of a damar picture varnish on a relatively fresh painting?*

A. Because it is useless to coat a painting with a concentrated varnish which will not last; the lighter retouching varnish is more satisfactory for this purpose.

192. *Q. Can one impart an even gloss to a fresh painting by using several applications of varnish?*

A. Not always, it is useless to varnish a fresh painting repeatedly; moreover, this will harm the glazes. The harder the paint film, the easier it is to produce an even gloss on its surface. Such a condition may prevail when a painting is several months or a few years old—depending on the thickness of the paint film, the climatic conditions, and the nature of the paint.

193. *Q. Should one apply the varnish generously or sparingly?*

A. Sparingly, always.

194. *Q. Should one use a mat varnish in order to obtain a dull paint surface?*

A. Mat varnishes as a rule are ineffective, since they contain wax which when polished (as will happen when dusting a painting) will become at once glossy.

195. *Q. Should beeswax be applied to a varnished surface and then polished?*

A. Wax always offers good protection to a dry varnish film.

196. *Q. How soon, and in what manner, should beeswax be applied to a varnished surface?*

A. Because wax is dissolved in turpentine or mineral spirits it should be used only on a well-dried paint surface. Wax should be distributed with a piece of lint-free linen or with a cheesecloth and left on the surface for an hour or more. Polishing with parallel horizontal strokes should then follow. (For wax, *see* Ch. 9.)

197. *Q. What brushes should one use for varnishing?*

A. A fresh painting should be varnished with a sable or other soft-hair brush because a soft surface may be injured by a stiff brush; glazes especially may be easily dissolved by careless varnishing. A well-dried painting can be varnished with a bristle brush, or a house-painter's brush of small size.

198. *Q. Should one use an atomizer for varnishing?*

A. No. Spraying deposits more varnish on a painting than is needed to obtain a cohesive paint film. A textured surface especially will accumulate in its declivities excessive amounts of varnish.

199. *Q. What can one do when, in spite of varnishing, some parts of a painting remain dull?*

A. When dull spots reappear on a varnished painting, this indicates that the paint surface has not solidified enough or that a loss of oil has occurred on certain parts of the paint film. Such spots can be oiled out with the copal painting medium thinned with turpentine in the proportion of 1:1.

200. *Q. Should one varnish a mat painting executed on an absorbent ground, or a painting executed with turpentine medium?*

A. No. Such paintings, because of their porous surfaces, are not likely to acquire gloss by varnishing.

201. *Q. How can one prevent trickling of varnish? (For trickling, see Q. 388.)*

A. To prevent this, before applying the varnish one should gently rub the paint surface with a piece of cotton slightly moistened.

202. *Q. Should one clean a painting before revarnishing?*

A. Dirt and old varnish should first be removed. (See Q. 418.)

203. *Q. How long does a varnish last when applied to a perfectly dry painting?*

A. This depends on the quality of the varnish and on climatic conditions. In a dry climate, a good damar varnish applied to a well-dried painting may last for two decades. Steam heat and moisture accelerate deterioration of resin varnishes.

204. *Q. Can one regenerate a brittle and fissured varnish film?*

A. Sometimes it is possible to fuse an originally strong varnish film by rubbing it gently with a piece of cotton moistened with mineral spirits, turpentine, or even benzene, and then polishing it with soft silk (silk stocking, for example).

205. *Q. Is it advisable to varnish paintings on very humid days?*

A. No, because a moist surface cannot be successfully varnished (especially when mastic is used). When moisture becomes arrested under the varnish, a bluish film appears, which is especially disturbing on the dark areas of a painting. This film is known as "bloom." (Q. 426, 427.)

206. *Q. How can one remove moisture from a paint surface before varnishing?*

A. On rainy days this is practically impossible— unless the room is heated. However, a careful warming up of the surface on which condensed moisture may have collected, plus a rubbing of it with a soft silk cloth (silk stockings), may help. (Obviously, the surface must not be overheated.)

207. *Q. Are varnishes which are prepared with synthetic resin suitable for use by the painter?*

A. Synthetic resin varnishes are often used today, and some of them are said, by reliable authorities, to be satisfactory. However, the addition of such a varnish to the painting medium is inadvisable because accurate data on the behavior of such varnishes with linseed oil have not yet been established.

BALSAMS (OLEO-RESINS)

208. *Q. What is a balsam?*

A. The general term refers to the resinous exudates

from coniferous trees; when obtained from the heart of certain kinds of needle trees, such as larch, balsams are known as venice turpentine, strasbourg turpentine, canada balsam, copaiba balsam. They are thick liquids of considerable viscosity and pleasant aromatic odor. Venice turpentine has been used at various times as an addition to the painting medium. Today, formulations calling for this ingredient are obsolete.

209. *Q. What is copaiba balsam?*

A. An exudate from certain coniferous trees found in Brazil and Venezuela. According to its source of origin, the quality and appearance of this balsam may vary considerably. It is entirely unsuitable as an addition to a painting medium because it tends to soften lower paint layers through its strong solving action. At one time this balsam was used as a panacea by restorers because to its penetrating action was ascribed the power to regenerate dried-up and brittle paint films. Today its value in this respect is discounted. However, it is still useful in connection with picture restoring. This balsam, when mixed with turpentine and left on the surface of a painting for a period of days, may soften an old oil varnish so as to make it more responsive to the action of various solvents such as benzene, acetone, alcohol.

PAINTING MEDIUM FORMULAS

210. *Q. Why is the presence of a varnish desirable in an oil medium used for thinning paints?*

A. When mixed with varnish (resin plus turpentine), (1) linseed oil becomes "leaner," (2) its tendency to yellow lessens, (3) its adhesive properties improve, (4) the brilliance and fusion of colors increase, (5) glazing and scumbling become practical, (6) overpainting is facilitated, (7) trickling is reduced. Straight linseed oil, on the other hand, has all the disadvantages of a fatty medium (the disadvantages become apparent only when overpainting, glazing, or scumbling).

211. *Q. What is the best proportion for a combination of oil and resin varnish?*

A. The larger the proportion of the soft resin (damar, mastic), the greater the danger, in time, of the film becoming brittle and remaining susceptible to the action of solvents such as turpentine or petroleum derivatives. Therefore, the oil should be present in the medium in sufficient quantities to protect the fragile resin. A viscous oil may be mixed with a larger proportion of the resin than a thin oil. Thus a heavy-body standoil or sun-thickened oil—thickened to the consistency of thick honey—can receive an addition of 50 per cent and the thin oil up to 25 per cent of copal varnish. By reasons of permanence it is not advisable to use damar varnish as part of the painting medium.

212. *Q. What are the nature, composition, and advantages of copal painting media and copal concentrate?*

A. (I refer here specifically to my own formulations as manufactured by Permanent Pigments, in Cincinnati, Ohio. The composition of other commercial copal preparations is not disclosed; therefore no statement on their quality and usability can be made.)

The Taubes Copal Painting Medium (Light) is a solution of water-white transparent congo copal in standoil, linseed oil and turpentine. Copal Painting Medium Heavy differs from the former only in the degree of viscosity, hence it is especially adapted for glazing. Both preparations are suitable for painting in thin, watercolor fashion and for painting in impasto. They are suitable for glazing, scumbling, overpainting, and they excel in elasticity, adhesive properties, permanence, and resistance to yellowing. Copal Concentrate is a solution of run copal in standoil. It is used in small amounts (a few drops mixed with the palette knife with 1 linear inch of paint as it comes from the tube). It provides the paint with more suppleness and generally creates textural effects such as we know them in the works of the early Flemish masters.

CHAPTER 9

Waxes

213. *Q. What is the nature of beeswax, and how is it used in painting?*

A. Beeswax is used as a suspension agent in the preparation of paint (Q. 300) and also for the protection of the surface of paintings (Q. 195). In combination with copal or damar varnish it forms an excellent emulsion for varnishing egg tempera panels. The U. S. P. variety, brownish in color, can be used for all purposes, although one can also obtain beeswax bleached to a white color. It can be instantly dissolved in hot turpentine or melted first and then mixed with warm turpentine. (Melting point of beeswax is 149° F.) It dissolves also in mineral spirits and other petrol derivatives without previous heating. A wax paste for polishing purposes should be prepared from 1 part beeswax (by weight) to 3 parts mineral spirits or turpentine (by fluid ounces) ; or 1½ parts turpentine and 1½ parts copal or damar varnish.

214. *Q. What is carnauba wax? How is it used?*

A. A wax obtained from the leaves of a Brazilian palm. It is harder than all other waxes, having a melting point of about 185° F. It is sold in colors ranging from light cream to dark brown. Carnauba wax should not be substituted for beeswax in preparation of paints, but it may well be used for protection of painting surfaces. In its natural state, carnauba wax is not soluble in turpentine or in petroleum derivatives, but, when melted, it can easily be compounded with solvents, especially with turpentine, for which it seems to have greater affinity than for mineral spirits. To prepare a workable paste, 1 part wax should be dissolved in about 3 parts turpentine and 3 parts of copal varnish.

215. *Q. What other waxes are on the market?*

A. Some better known waxes are: refined petroleum products such as paraffin wax (melting point 125° F. to 140° F., depending on the grade) ; ozokerite (earth wax found in Boryslav, Galizia. Melting point 142° F. to 173° F.) ; and ceresin, which is refined from the former; it is sometimes used as a substitute for beeswax, which it resembles.

CHAPTER 10

Miscellaneous Materials

216. *Q. What is aluminum stearate?*

A. A metallic soap used in the preparation of paints as a stabilizer (Q. 299). Its presence in the body of a paint prevents oil and pigment separation (Q. 297) ; also it causes the consistency and the resulting brushability of paint to change to such an extent that even a stringy paint becomes short and buttery.

217. *Q. What qualities of aluminum stearate are useful as stabilizers?*

A. There are various grades of the material, depending on their manufacturing source; therefore in obtaining aluminum stearate from different sources, differences of behavior may be noted. Only the mono- and di- forms of aluminum stearate are of value to the painter.

218. *Q. How can aluminum stearate be incorporated with paint?*

A. *See* Question 302.

219. *Q. Should aluminum stearate be mixed with paint which is ground for a few days' use; that is, when the paint is not put into tubes?*

A. No. Only certain tube colors should receive it (Q. 307).

220. *Q. What is clay?*

A. Clay, also known as China clay, or kaolin, is an

aluminum silicate formed by the decomposition of feldspar. Any presence of color in the clay (which, as a rule, is a white or slightly yellowish pigment) indicates the presence of iron oxide or other minerals. Clay is present in ochre (American) in amounts up to 80 per cent; also in iron oxide reds, umber, sienna, and green earth. However, the best qualities of French or English ochre contain more silica (quartz) than clay. Silica, which is crystalline in structure as compared with the amorphous clay, renders the ochre more opaque. Both silica and clay are present in varying amounts in all the earth colors. Depending on their place of origin, they come in various textures from fine to coarse.

221. *Q. What are the uses of clay in painting?*

A. Clay which is not too coarse can be added to the dense, opaque iron oxides as a stabilizer; also to certain mars colors which have a strong tendency to separate from oil, but will remain in perfect suspension in the presence of clay. Clay can be added to such pigments in amounts ranging up to 10 per cent without noticeably impairing the tinting strength of these pigments (*see* Q. 303). Clay, as well as silica, may also be added to the paint used for priming; the coarser quality is particularly adapted for this purpose because it imparts tooth to the painting ground.

222. *Q. What are the uses of green earth pigment?*

A. It can be used instead of aluminum stearate or clay as a stabilizer in grinding paint.

223. *Q. What is aluminum hydrate?*

A. It is a base for dyes such as alizarin crimson and hansa yellow. The transparent, colorless material is often used as a paint adulterant.

224. *Q. What preservatives are used to prevent gum, glue, or casein solutions, and egg emulsions from decomposing?*

A. Phenol (carbolic acid) is a standard germicide. It should be used in a 10 per cent solution, 1 per cent of which should be added as a preservative. (That is, about 1 teaspoonful should be added to 14 ounces of the liquid to be preserved.) Dowcide is a compound produced by the Dow Chemical Company. One teaspoonful of the powder should be added to 1 pint of the liquid. Methyl alcohol, known as methanol (Q. 151), may also be used, but because it evaporates from the solution, it is a short-lived preservative.

CHAPTER **11**

Pigments and Oil Paints

225. *Q. What is the difference between pigment and paint?*

A. Pigment refers to the dry color matter; when mixed with oil (known as a "vehicle") pigment becomes oil paint.

226. *Q. Are European-made oil colors better than those produced in the United States?*

A. Since the content of a tube of color prepared abroad is never stated on the label, it is reasonable to assume that domestic paints will be in many cases superior, that is, provided the manufacturer adheres to the provisions laid down by the Bureau of Standards (C.S. 2926). According to this provision, the contents of a tube should always appear on the label. So, for instance, naples yellow should carry a line, "lead antimoniate," and cobalt blue, "cobalt oxide," etc.

227. *Q. Which pigments are produced in the United States and which are imported?*

A. Of all of the colors mentioned in this book, only the best grade earth colors come from abroad. All the other pigments are manufactured in the United States and, according to reliable tests, their quality at least equals, and often surpasses, that of the best foreign products.

228. *Q. In what way do cheap colors differ from expensive ones?*

A. As a rule, cheap paint is cut with fillers, or may even consist of dye precipitated on a base such as barium sulphate, aluminum hydrate, etc. The cheap product may also contain impurities and may be prepared with an inferior oil.

229. *Q. Does stronger tint of a color always indicate superior quality?*

A. Not necessarily; sometimes an otherwise too-dull color may have been strengthened by the addition of a dye.

230. *Q. How does one test the tinting of a color?*

A. This is carried out by the volumetric reduction of paint. A small quantity of the color to be tested is mixed with 10 times its measure of white lead or zinc white. When comparing a color thus reduced with another sample which has been likewise reduced, the stronger tint will point to a more powerful pigment.

231. *Q. Which of the more popular colors still available on the market should be avoided?*

A. Ultramarine, green and cobalt green, rose madder; although permanent, are exceedingly weak and therefore next to useless. Vandyke brown (asphaltum, cassel brown), carmine, harrison red, indigo, and emerald green are impermanent.

232. *Q. Why do some paints harden in tubes after prolonged storage, and some others become oily and thin?*

A. Hardening of paint is, as a rule, the result of pigment and oil separation; also, chemical reaction may bring about solidification of a paint. When a paint becomes too thin, the indication is that too much oil was used in its preparation.

233. *Q. Why do some commercial colors remain limpid in tubes, whereas some of the self-prepared paints, in spite of the addition of a suspension agent, become hard?*

A. The incorporation of the suspension agent by high pressure, as in factory production, is more efficient.

234. *Q. How can a color which has solidified in a tube be made usable again?*

A. It all depends on the cause of this condition. When oil and pigments separate, the paint can be taken out of the tube and re-ground with a quantity of fresh oil and an addition of 1 per cent of aluminum stearate or green earth or wax (Q. 301, 302). When paint has jellified—that is, turned to a rubbery, liver-like substance—regrinding is useless because of the chemical changes in the oil-pigment compound.

235. *Q. How long does a color remain usable when kept in a tube?*

A. In air-tight tubes, commercial paint containing stabilizer will be preserved indefinitely.

236. *Q. How can one improve paint which has become too thin?*

A. Place it on an absorbent paper—for example, newspaper— which will draw the excess oil from the paint.

237. *Q. Which is preferable as far as permanence of painting is concerned, thin paint or paint poor in oil?*

A. Neither. There is an optimum of oil-absorption for every pigment. An excess of oil may cause a color to yellow, and lack of enough oil may cause it to become brittle and crack.

238. *Q. Which colors are more inclined to yellow?*

A. The white and the blue colors.

EARTH COLORS

239. *Q. What is the composition of earth pigments?*

A. Earth pigments are mixtures of clay, silica, and coloring matter, such as various forms of iron oxide, and manganese dioxide. They also contain impurities, chiefly gypsum and magnesium carbonate.

240. *Q. Are earth colors permanent?*

A. Providing they are properly washed (i.e., purified) they possess greatest permanence.

241. *Q. What is the drying capacity of the earth colors?*

A. Ochre, venetian red, and indian red dry moderately well; sienna, which contains some manganese dioxide, dries better; and umber, with up to 16 per cent of manganese dioxide, is the most rapid drier of all our paints.

242. *Q. What can be said as to the body and opacity of the earth colors?*

A. Depending on quality and place of origin, their

texture is more or less coarse. Because of the clay content, these colors are, as a rule, also short. (It takes a relatively large amount of polymerized oil to produce a stringy quality in an earth color.) Opacity of earth colors varies: raw sienna, gold ochre, and green earth are transparent; burnt sienna is semi-transparent; yellow ochres are moderately opaque; and venetian red, indian red, and umber are opaque.

243. *Q. Is the tinting capacity of earth colors strong or weak?*

A. It is exceedingly weak in green earth; moderate in raw sienna and ochres; strong in burnt sienna, venetian red, umber, indian red, and the deepest variety of purple-red (known as caput mortuum in Europe and the mars violet in the United States).

MARS COLORS

244. *Q. What are the mars colors and how do they compare with the earth colors?*

A. Mars colors are artificial earth colors. They are just as permanent as earth colors, but differ from them in the following respects. Mars yellow is more transparent than ochre, possesses greater tinting strength, and its color is more intensely yellow. Mars orange is still more transparent and resembles raw sienna. Darker varieties of ochre cannot be replaced by any of the mars colors.

Mars red sometimes comes in a very light tint, resembling a terra di pozzuoli (a name for a light red mined in the village of Pozzuoli in the neighborhood of Naples); when mixed with white it yields a bright, cold pink. A darker shade of mars red becomes violet when mixed with white, just as do some darker shades of venetian red (so-called english red) when mixed with white. Mars reds harden to a tougher consistency than natural iron oxides, and their drying capacity is better.

245. *Q. What is the difference between caput mortuum and mars violet (Permanent Pigments make)?*

A. The two colors possess an almost identical hue; however, the mars color dries quicker and to a harder film than the natural earth color.

246. *Q. What other mars colors can be used in painting?*

A. Mars brown and mars brown dark. The first is much more red than burnt umber, and the second resembles the color of a chocolate. Both colors have exceptional tinting strength, excellent drying capacity, and they harden to an exceedingly tough and elastic film. Unlike umber, they produce strongly violet hues in mixtures with white.

247. *Q. Is mars black a good substitute for ivory black?*

A. No. Its tinting strength is considerably greater, but its color is not as deep. In mixtures with white, mars black turns to a grey-violet. It dries by far better than ivory black and its film is much tougher. (Therefore, it can very well be used for impasto painting.)

WHITE COLORS

248. *Q. Is it true that white lead (always designated as flake white when in tubes) oil paint yellows and turns black, and also that it affects adversely certain other colors?*

A. In practice, these alleged deficiencies of white lead are non-existent. White lead blackens in the presence of sulphurated air, but this condition does not exist in environments where people live and work, that is, not sufficiently to affect the color of white lead.

249. *Q. Does white lead become yellow when exposed to darkness and moisture?*

A. When kept away from daylight, a white lead application, especially if fresh, will yellow; this condition will be aggravated in the presence of moisture. A well-dried color will be much less affected by such adverse conditions. Bleaching of a yellowed paint can be carried out by exposing it to strong daylight for a period of several weeks or shorter exposures to indirect sunlight. (For bleaching paintings, *see* Q. 425.)

250. *Q. Is white lead poisonous?*

A. When the dry powder is inhaled, or when the paint is brought in contact with open wounds, or when food becomes contaminated with it, frequent intake of white lead is injurious. According to medical advice, continued intake of milk neutralizes the presence of white lead in the human body.

251. *Q. What makes white lead a superior pigment?*

A. Its outstanding qualities are: low oil absorption, great density, opacity, excellent drying quality, firm body, and exceptional capacity for solidifying admixtures of oil.

252. *Q. What qualities account for the fact that white lead possesses a better body than any of the other white pigments?*

A. The particle size of white lead is more than twice that of titanium oxide or zinc white. This means that all the other white pigments are much more finely divided than white lead.

253. *Q. What is saponification of white lead?*

A. Because of the acidity which linseed oil develops while drying, lead hydroxide (a part of the white lead molecule) partially saponifies the oil, with which it forms a homogeneous, extremely durable and elastic paint film; its opacity, however, suffers to some extent under this condition.

254. *Q. How does white lead react when mixed with polymerized oil or with oil of a high acid value?*

A. The pigment is very susceptible to change in its characteristics, depending on the quality of oil. A neutral oil will make it "short." But even an oil of a moderately high acid value will make it somewhat stringy and "long." A heat processed oil will impart enamel-like quality to the pigment.

255. *Q. How can a "short" white lead be changed to a "long" one?*

A. Add to the paint a small quantity of Copal Concentration (see Q. 212).

256. *Q. What is the difference between white lead, flake white, and Cremnitz white?*

A. The first two are identical. Cremnitz white, because of a slight variation in its manufacturing process, possesses a whiter color but is less opaque.

257. *Q. Can the white lead sold in cans be used in painting?*

A. Although the pigment used in canned paint is identical to that contained in tube paint, the canned white lead yellows more because it is ground in a different manner than the artist's color. (For canned white lead, *see also* Q. 26.)

258. *Q. What are the advantages of mixing oil white with tempera white?*

A. The so-called "mixed" white dries more quickly. However, because of its relative brittleness, it should not be used in pastose applications on canvas.

259. *Q. Are titanium white paints reliable, and what is their composition?*

A. Present-day titanium white mixtures are inert

and permanent. They are chiefly composed of titanium oxide, precipitated on barium sulphate, or mixtures of titanium white, zinc white, etc.

260. *Q. What are the merits of titanium white?*

A. Reflection of white light, opacity, tinting strength, and hiding power of the titanium color are greater than those of any other white paint. Also, it is not inclined to yellow.

261. *Q. What makes titanium white inferior to white lead?*

A. It possesses a much finer body, dries slowly, and its oil absorption is higher than that of white lead. Moreover, since it is a modern color, its behavior over a period of centuries is unknown. In mixtures with other colors, its great tinting capacity is not always an advantage, as it greatly reduces the strength of these colors.

262. *Q. What tones does titanium oxide yield in mixtures with other colors?*

A. As compared with white lead, it produces, like zinc white, much colder hues.

263. *Q. What are the principal characteristics of zinc white?*

A. It is whiter and colder in color than white lead, and it yellows less. On the other hand, its hiding and drying powers are inferior, and its oil absorption is almost twice that of white lead. Also, it dries to a hard, rather brittle film, its brittleness increasing with age.

264. *Q. When is the use of zinc white appropriate?*

A. When a slow-drying paint is required, zinc white, ground in poppy oil, might be considered.

265. *Q. How does zinc white influence other colors?*

A. Like titanium white, it yields cooler, more chalky tones. For example, ivory black mixed with white lead will appear as a warm gray, as compared to a bluish gray resulting from a mixture of zinc white and ivory black.

266. *Q. Should zinc white be used for underpainting?*

A. No. It is brittle, contains too much oil and lacks sufficient opacity. It is also liable to crack when used in lower layers.

BLUE COLORS

267. *Q. How do prussian blue, ultramarine blue, cerulean blue, cobalt blue, and manganese blue differ one from another?*

A. Prussian blue has the most powerful tinting strength; manganese blue is the weakest. Both are transparent (however, the strong tint of prussian blue neutralizes to an extent this quality); they are the best dryers of all the blue colors. Ultramarine blue is also transparent, and the only one possessing a violet hue. Cerulean blue is the only opaque blue on our palette. It is a good dryer and, when genuine, its tinting strength is good and its color is useful in painting atmospheric effects. Cobalt blue, as compared with ultramarine, has little transparency, and its color is rather sweet.

268. *Q. What other blue color can be used?*

A. Phthalocyanine blue (monastral blue) is a more recently developed color; it resembles prussian blue, with which it shares great tinting strength, but lacks the excellent drying capacity, firm texture, and the peculiar greenish cast of the latter. Monastral colors are absolutely permanent.

269. *Q. How should one use prussian blue?*

A. It is generally used as an addition to other colors because its strong tinting capacity radically changes the hue of any other color or color combination. It is especially useful in obtaining green tints. Because of its quick-drying quality, it is well adapted for use in underpainting.

270. *Q. How should one use ultramarine?*

A. Without admixture of a body color, it should be used only as a glaze. When applied with impasto, it takes on a blackish appearance. When mixed with red colors, ultramarine yields violet nuances.

271. *Q. How should one use cerulean and cobalt blue?*

A. When an opaque blue of a greenish cast is required, cerulean blue can become a desirable color.

272. *Q. How should one use manganese blue?*

A. Chiefly as a dryer. Because of its weak tint it is best to mix it with equally weak colors, such as barium yellow.

RED COLORS

273. *Q. How do the the red colors—cadmium red, vermilion, venetian red, indian red, mars violet, alizarin crimson, and burnt sienna—differ one from another?*

A. With the exception of alizarin crimson and burnt sienna, which are transparent colors, and cadmium red, which is moderately opaque, they all possess extreme opacity. Cadmium, vermilion, and alizarin crimson are very slow dryers. The most brilliant reds are vermilion and cadmium red; burnt sienna also yields a fiery red hue when applied as a glaze on a bright underpainting. In thick layers it appears as a dull brown-red.

274. *Q. How should one use the red colors?*

A. When mixed with white, red colors turn to pink or to violet. This implies that a lighter hue of red color cannot be produced by admixtures of white. However, cadmium yellow will brighten the hue of the dull red colors. Vermilion, because of its firm texture, is more suitable for pastose application than cadmium red. All the other iron oxide colors may also be applied in a pastose manner, but alizarin crimson, when used without admixtures of other body paints, is a typical glazing color. Venetian red is the proper term for an artificial iron oxide. As such it has an enormous tinting strength. Much milder, natural iron oxides are: light red, terra di pozzuoli, terra rosa. (Q. 286, 287.)

YELLOW COLORS

275. *Q. How do the yellow colors differ one from another?*

A. Of the yellow colors, naples yellow is the most opaque, hansa and barium yellow the most transparent. Cadmium yellows possess brilliant hues, and naples and barium yellow are comparatively pale. Zinc yellow has a greenish cast, and ochre is a brown-yellow. Cadmium yellows and barium yellow are finely divided pigments and they are all poor dryers; naples yellow is also a fine-textured pigment, but it dries faster than any of the other yellow colors.

276. *Q. When should one use barium yellow?*

A. Mostly for atmospheric effects. Where naples yellow proves to be too strong, barium yellow can take its place.

277. *Q. When does one use naples yellow?*

A. Mostly for pastose and opaque applicatons in backgrounds and for atmospheric effects. Because it is a lead color (lead antimoniate), it behaves not unlike white lead in mixtures with other colors.

278. *Q. When should one use zinc yellow?*

A. In mixtures where cadmium appears to be too powerful, zinc yellow may take its place. Also, in instances where a "long" color is required, it will be most useful. One should consider, however, that it turns slightly greenish in time; since it is used chiefly for green mixtures, this is entirely unobjectionable. When combined with blues it produces a cool bluish-green, thus suggesting that it contains a white pigment (zinc oxide).

279. *Q. When should one use cadmium yellow and cadmium orange?*

A. Where a strong yellow or a green tint is required, cadmium yellow is the most important color on our palette. The cadmiums are suitable for glazing, as well as for opaque painting. Cadmium orange stands between cadmium yellow and cadmium red. It may be obtained from the mixture of cadmium red and cadmium yellow. In mixtures with white, cadmium orange shows the characteristics of cadmium red; that is, a violet cast appears in it. (For cadmium red, *see* Q. 273, 274.)

280. *Q. When should one use hansa yellow?*

A. This color, which has the tint of a bright cadmium yellow, is entirely transparent and possesses great tinting strength. Because it is prepared from a dye, it should be used only as a glaze, and in small additions to influence other colors. (*See* lakes, Q. 286.)

281. *Q. What is the difference between a cadmium sulphide and a cadmium-barium paint?*

A. The straight cadmium sulphides, in spite of their greater tinting strength, are otherwise not considered superior to the modern and much cheaper product which is a co-precipitated mixture of cadmium sulphide and barium sulphate.

GREEN COLORS

282. *Q. What is the difference between viridian green (chrome oxide green transparent), monastral green (phthalocyanine), and chrome oxide green opaque?*

A. The first two are similar in tint, but monastral green is more brilliant, transparent, and possesses a far greater tinting power. Both are excellent glazing colors. Chrome oxide green opaque, on the other hand, is extremely dense, and because of its great tinting strength, an excellent color to cope with other strong paints such as the iron oxide reds.

BROWN COLORS

283. *Q. What is the difference between raw and burnt umber and the mars browns?*

A. Raw umber has a cool brown cast, and the latter a darker, warm reddish-brown color. The umbers and mars browns, although they do not differ much when superficially compared, are quite dissimilar, and cannot very well be substituted one for another. The radical difference becomes apparent at once in mixtures with other colors, and especially with white. Although mars browns are not quite as good dryers as umber, they solidify throughout to a much tougher, and at the same time elastic, film. Therefore, they are better adapted to pastose painting than the umber.

284. *Q. How could one approximate the shade of umber for use in instances where a slower drying color is desired.*

A. To match the shade of umber, mix ivory black, burnt sienna, and dark ochre. In mixtures with other colors and with white, this mixed paint will, from a coloristic standpoint, behave not much differently from umber.

BLACK COLORS

285. *Q. How should one use ivory black, and mars black?*

A. Where a pastose application is contemplated, the use of ivory black should be avoided; because of its poor drying properties it remains wet within for a very long time, whereas mars black dries throughout to a tough film in a comparatively short time. Mars black also has a much stronger tinting capacity. Ivory black possesses greater depth, finer texture, and is more transparent.

THE LAKES

286. *Q. What is a lake color?*

A. A dye precipitated on a colorless base such as, for example, aluminum hydrate (Q. 223). Alizarin crimson, hansa yellow, and the monastral colors are such paints.

287. *Q. What is the difference between madder lake and alizarin crimson?*

A. The first is a natural product obtained from the root of the madder plant; the second is an aniline dye.

288. *Q. Which of the two is preferable?*

A. Although the hue of both colors is identical, the synthetic product, which has replaced the former almost completely, is said to be the more permanent. It is also the more powerful of the two. However, the true madder color is still produced by some firms.

SELECTING COLORS

289. *Q. What colors should a beginner use to familiarize himself with the palette?*

A. White lead, ultramarine blue, prussian blue, viridian green, yellow ochre, cadmium yellow, cadmium orange, cadmium red, venetian red, indian red, alizarin crimson, burnt sienna, burnt umber, ivory black.

290. *Q. What colors might be added to the above list?*

A. Chrome oxide green dull, cerulean blue, cobalt blue, manganese blue, monastral blue, monastral green, naples yellow, mars yellow, barium yellow, zinc yellow, strontium yellow, hansa yellow, raw umber, vermilion, mars brown, mars black, mars violet.

291. *Q. In what manner should the colors be arranged on the palette?*

A. Place white in the middle of the palette; it is practical to group the blues and the greens to the right, and the yellows, reds, browns, and black, to the left.

CHAPTER 12

Grinding Pigments by Hand

292. *Q. What is the advantage of a studio-prepared paint over the commercial product?*

A. The body and consistency of certain self-prepared colors can, because of the choice of a particular oil, or the omission of aluminum stearate, be rendered different from that of the commercial paint.

293. *Q. Is the uniform brushability of commercial paint an advantage, and how is this brought about?*

A. For the beginner, or the painter who does not want to be bothered with the exploration of his paint, the uniform consistency of paints is desirable. This uniformly short consistency is achieved by the addition of a stabilizer (definition, Q. 297), usually aluminum stearate. (For aluminum stearate, *see* Q. 299.)

294. *Q. Are the machine-prepared colors finer than those ground by hand?*

A. The pigments come already finely ground. As a rule, the particle size of the pigments is not reduced by grinding, but the particle aggregates are more thoroughly dispersed in the oil when mechanical means are used.

295. *Q. Which hand-ground paints have the consistency of the commercial product, and which may be influenced by the painter?*

A. The earth colors, prussian blue, the cadmiums, and all the colors prepared from dyes are similar in character when prepared either by hand or by mechanical means. The rest of the colors in the palette can be changed radically, from short to long.

296. *Q. What are the causes of changes in the consistency of paint?*

A. The size and shape of the pigment particles; the acidity or polymerization of oil with which the pigments are mixed; the difference in stabilizers with which commercial paints are prepared.

297. *Q. What is a stabilizer and why is one used in preparation of paint?*

A. Some pigments do not remain in suspension with oil; they tend to separate after days, weeks, or months. Therefore, when storage in tubes is contemplated, these paints must receive the addition of a stabilizer in order to remain in usable condition for long periods of time. (Q. 299.)

298. *Q. In general, should one use stabilizers when grinding paints for immediate use?*

A. No. Only mars yellow and, especially, mars orange, will separate from its vehicle in a few days.

299. *Q. Which are the most frequently used stabilizers and in what quantity should they be used?*

A. In commercial paints aluminum stearate (Q. 306, 309) is chiefly used. It generally supersedes beeswax (Q. 303). A stabilizer can be added to the paint in the amount of up to 2 per cent of its total weight. (That is, oil plus pigment.)

300. *Q. When is the addition of beeswax required in paint?*

A. Wax, like aluminum stearate, tends to soften

the paint film. Certain pigments which are brittle by nature improve with the addition of wax. Viridian green and ultramarine blue are such colors. Ultramarine may also harden in tubes after storage of a year or more. Prussian blue is inclined to become granulated, but wax will counteract this tendency.

301. *Q. How should one combine wax with paint?*

A. Dissolve ¼ ounce of beeswax in about 3 teaspoonfuls of hot turpentine and mix it with 16 ounces of hot linseed oil. Grind the pigments in this compound while it is hot. When the medium cools, the wax will separate from it, but when re-heated it will again form a solution. (It is best to use a mortar for this purpose because it can easily be kept warm. A pestle will serve for grinding the pigment.)

302. *Q. How should one incorporate aluminum stearate with paint?*

A. Moisten aluminum stearate slightly with alcohol, and add enough water to mix it to a stiff paste. Add the paste to the paint and mull it thoroughly together. (Q. 307.) (Aluminum stearate is water-repellent; it must, therefore, first be moistened with alcohol in order to accept water.)

303. *Q. What other stabilizers may be used?*

A. Clay may be added to opaque colors and to colors that have a rather coarse body. Iron oxides, such as venetian red, indian red, caput mortuum, and the mars colors, can receive up to 10 per cent of clay without loss of tinting capacity. In my own practice, I have come to use raw green earth (pigment) as a stabilizing agent. It can be added in a quantity up to about 20 per cent (by bulk) to most of the colors requiring a stabilizer. Because of its weak tinting strength, green earth will not affect the hue of any color to an appreciable extent.

304. *Q. How should one incorporate green earth or clay with paint?*

A. First mix the required quantity of these pigments with oil to a stiff paste and mull it thoroughly. Then mix the paste with a small quantity of the paint and mull it; add some more paint and mull once more, continuing to add the rest of the paint gradually.

305. *Q. What will be the result of excessive use—or lack— of aluminum stearate or beeswax in paint?*

A. In the first instance, the paint film will become too soft. In the second, the paint may separate from the oil and harden in the tube after prolonged storage.

306. *Q. Can a color which has hardened in the tube because of pigment and oil separation be made usable again?*

A. As in the case of the commercial product (*see* Q. 234), the studio-prepared paint can be taken out of the tube and re-ground with fresh oil and some stabilizer.

307. *Q. Which colors tend to harden in tubes and therefore require the addition of a stabilizer?*

A. Cerulean blue, manganese blue, venetian red, indian red, mars yellow, mars orange, mars red, mars violet, mars brown, vermilion. Some qualities of the cadmium sulphides and selenides also need the admixture of a stabilizer.

PAINT CONSISTENCY

308. *Q. Which colors have a tendency to become brittle?*

A. Barium yellow, zinc yellow, ultramarine blue, viridian green. Alizarin crimson and ivory black, although they do not become brittle in a strict sense, are greatly improved by an addition of polymerized oil.

309. *Q. Which colors have a tendency to become stringy?*

A. Naples yellow, zinc yellow, mars yellow, mars brown, mars black, prussian blue, white lead.

310. *Q. Which paints do not need a stabilizer?*

A. Zinc white, white lead, the ochres, the siennas, umber, viridian green, prussian blue, chrome oxide green opaque, mars black, ivory black, all the lake colors.

311. *Q. How can one change a short color to a long color?*

A. An addition of Copal Concentrate will change the body of the paint. Also, when paints on the palette are exposed to the action of air, they will develop free acids after days or weeks—depending on their characteristics. After removing the skin which forms on them, the paint within will be stringy. However, not all paints will react in this manner. Paints containing much clay or stabilizer may remain short.

312. *Q. Which colors are short by nature?*

A. Viridian green, cadmiums, the earth colors, ochre, the siennas, red oxides, umbers, ivory black, and all the precipitated paints, such as monastral blue and green, hansa yellow, alizarin crimson.

GRINDING TOOLS

313. *Q. What instruments should be used for grinding paints?*

A. A ground plate glass at least 20 inches square and a muller with a grinding surface of about 2½ to 3 inches.

314. *Q. How should one impart tooth to the plate glass and the muller?*

A. Place on the plate a tablespoonful of carborundum grain, mesh No. 40; mix it with a little water, and rotate the muller for a few minutes on the surface of the plate. Replace the worn-out carborundum with a fresh quantity and continue grinding until the entire glass surface has been roughened.

315. *Q. How often should the plate glass be re-ground?*

A. After grinding some 10 to 20 ounces of pigment, depending on the pigment's hardness, the tooth of the glass and the muller may wear out.

316. *Q. How does one free the grinding tools from paint that clings to them?*

A. First moisten the paint with petroleum, then use soap and water.

GRINDING OIL

317. *Q. What kind of oil should be used for grinding?*

A. When short paint is required, the oil should possess a low acid number. For long quality of paint, oil of higher acid number should be used. For pigments which are apt to produce brittle films, addition of standoil is recommended.

318. *Q. Should a pigment be ground in thickened oil?*

A. When mixed with heat-treated oil, most pigments take on the character of enamel paint; they tend to level off and do not leave brush marks. Such paint is rarely suitable for painting. Moreover, it has a tendency to wrinkle and to remain wet for a long time underneath the thick skin which forms on it while drying. However, small amounts of a thickened oil can be added to colors such as ivory black, alizarin crimson, barium yellow, zinc yellow.

319. *Q. Should pigment be ground in a resinous vehicle in case one wishes to paint with a resinous medium?*

A. When paint is prepared for immediate use, some

Copal Concentrate (Q. 212) should be added (Q. 185). When paint is prepared for storage in tubes, addition of resin is inadvisable because some pigments react with it and eventually congeal.

320. *Q. How much oil is needed to prepare a pigment?*

A. The quantity of oil varies not only with different colors, but also with different grades of pigment. Depending on manufacturing methods, pigments representing identical colors have high or low oil absorption.

321. *Q. Should paint be of thin or thick consistency?*

A. Paint should be neither too poor nor too rich in oil. The first condition brings about brittleness of the paint film. Upon drying, such a film may rub off because its particles are not bound with a sufficient quantity of oil. A paint which is too thin cannot be used for impasto; its stability may also suffer.

322. *Q. How can one determine the proper quantity of oil needed to prepare a color?*

A. When a paint which is at first stiff loosens up after prolonged mulling, its consistency should be such as to offer normal brushability. Difficult brushability may point to an insufficient amount of oil, insufficient grinding, or to high acidity of the oil.

323. *Q. Which colors may receive more oil, as needed, to produce normal brushability?*

A. Viridian green, ultramarine, and barium yellow gain in elasticity when prepared with an excess of binder. Prussian blue may also be ground to a somewhat looser consistency.

GRINDING PIGMENTS

324. *Q. How should the hand grinding of pigments with oil proceed?*

A. First, a small quantity of pigment—about 2 or 3 teaspoonfuls at a time—should be mixed with oil to a stiff paste with a strong palette knife. Then the muller (Q. 313) should be used. A paste which appears dense and brittle at first will, under prolonged mulling, become lustrous and much thinner. Depending on the pigment, a quantity of 2 or 3 teaspoonfuls may require up to 8 minutes of mulling before the particle aggregates are well dispersed in the vehicle.

325. *Q. Should one use a palette knife for grinding colors?*

A. Unless used forcefully a palette knife does not sufficiently divide the particle aggregate of a pigment; a paint which is not well dispersed in oil will remain brittle. Small quantities of pigment can be ground with a stiff, strong knife. There is no danger of over-grinding when using the mulling method. Machine-ground paint may be overground at times, although a carefully prepared commercial color as a rule does not show such a fault.

326. *Q. How much pigment and oil would fill a studio tube?*

A. (Unless otherwise specified, the numbers stand for teaspoonfuls. The quantities of the white colors refer to a one-pound tube.) Ultramarine 17, oil 7; cerulean blue 12, oil 6; prussian blue 14, oil 8; viridian green 11, oil 8; chrome oxide green dull 15, oil 6; yellow ochre 18, oil 5; mars yellow 16, oil 9; zinc yellow 20, oil 7; naples yellow 16, oil 6; barium yellow 20, oil 7; cadmium yellow 21, oil 6; cadmium red 20, oil 6; burnt umber 15, oil 9; mars brown 20, oil 9; burnt sienna 12, oil 8; light red 20, oil 11; indian red 12, oil 9; alizarin crimson 16, oil 7; vermilion 15, oil 8; ivory black 13, oil 7; mars black 24, oil 7; white lead 18 ounces, oil 2½ fluid ounces; zinc white 10 ounces, oil 3 fluid ounces.

327. *Q. How should one fill a tube with paint?*

A. Fill the tube from the bottom, using a palette

knife. The paint should be put in a small amount at a time, in order to permit it to settle down without leaving air pockets. Continuous tapping of the screw end of the tube on the palm of the hand is necessary to promote the settling of the paints. About 1 inch of the tube should be left for folding. To close a tube properly, fold the flattened metal and then fold it again in the opposite direction.

328. *Q. How can one prevent paint from drying up when storing it in glass jars?*

A. Place thin cellophane or wax paper on top of the paint and pour enough linseed oil on it to prevent the access of air.

329. *Q. Can one pour water on top of the paint (stored in jars) to prevent it from drying out?*

A. Only white lead may be covered with water. Most of the other paints may suffer in presence of water.

330. *Q. How can one keep paint from drying out on the palette?*

A. Quantities of oil paint can be kept fresh on a palette for several weeks if tightly covered with pieces of thin cellophane or tinfoil.

CHAPTER 13

Simple Tests of Paints and Pigments

This chapter was written to help those painters who may wish to satisfy themselves as to the nature of their colors. Since painters as a rule are not trained to conduct complicated chemical analyses, only the simplest methods have been described. The equipment suggested is quite modest, but sufficient to conduct the tests with little difficulty.

MATERIALS AND EQUIPMENT FOR CONDUCTING SIMPLE TESTS

Apparatus: A delicate balance, beaker, test tubes, blow-pipe, charcoal, crucible, Bunsen burner, filter (should be alkali-resistant), funnel.

Chemicals: Caustic solution (2 tablespoonfuls of lye to 1 quart of water), hydrochloric acid, nitric acid, aqua regia, ammonium hydroxide, washing soda (soda crystals).

331. *Q. Are commercial tube paints, as a rule, correctly labeled as to their content?*

A. Unless the content of a tube is specified on the label, and the manufacturer states that he complies with the Commercial Standards (C.S. 2926) accepted by the National Bureau of Standards, it may be in some instances assumed that the more expensive pigments used do not conform to this standard but have been extended with inferior materials. (Foreign manufacturers do not state the contents of the tube on their labels; therefore, when a supposedly expensive paint is sold at a low figure, one can be fairly certain that the original pigment has been adulterated or that substitutes have been used.)

332. *Q. Which paints are most likely to be mislabeled?*

A. Cerulean blue, cobalt blue, naples yellow, vermilion, the pure cadmium sulphides, and cadmium selenides.

333. *Q. In what manner can a paint be adulterated?*

A. A paint can be cut with fillers; or a dye precipitated on a base of barytes, aluminum hydrate, clay, etc., may be substituted for the original pigment. Also, the original pigment can be "improved" or "enhanced" with a dye. In the first case, the tinting power of the color is reduced and the oil absorption altered, hence the behavior of the paint is changed and its permanence jeopardized. When a paint is made up of a precipitated dye, it may appear even more powerful than that produced from an original pigment; but its permanence will be dubious because only a few of the organic dyes are considered absolutely permanent. Moreover, a precipitated pigment will, in mixtures with other colors, produce different tints from those obtained from mixtures of pure pigments.

334. *Q. How can one ascertain for oneself whether a paint is adulterated with a filler?*

A. The tests may be made either by volumetric reduction (Q. 230) or chemical reaction. The volumetric reduction test may not always be reliable because, in addition to the filler, a paint may contain a dye which strengthens its color. To detect the presence and the approximate quantity of an insoluble filler (such as kaolin, barytes, etc.) by a chemical process, the following general method may be used: Weigh a small amount of the pigment and boil it with a caustic; then wash residue with water to remove caustic. Boil with aqua regia. Dilute this mixture with distilled water 1:10. Filter. Dry this residue and weigh it. Multiply the weight of the residue by the weight of the original material to find the percentage of the insoluble filler.

335. *Q. What materials will dissolve in nitric acid, hydrochloric acid, or aqua regia?*

A. Whiting and calcium carbonate will reveal their presence by dissolving under effervescence.

336. *Q. How can one test a paint (inorganic pigment) for the presence of an organic dye?*

A. An organic dye (usually a coal tar color) can be extracted from the paint (or the pigment). The paint is stirred in a beaker with alcohol or benzene and then filtered. If the color filters through, this indicates the presence of a dye. Colors containing a water-soluble dye can be treated with water. (Organic dyes should always be removed before making chemical tests on a pigment for the presence of metals.)

337. *Q. What is the blow-pipe test?*

A. Some colors may be submitted to a blow-pipe test, as follows: The paint is placed in a small scoop made in a piece of charcoal and burned with the help of a blow-pipe. After a few minutes the organic dye burns off but the base consisting of the white inert filler remains unchanged.

338. *Q. What other facts can be brought out by the blow-pipe test?*

A. White lead when subjected to the test will be reduced entirely into metallic lead. If it contains any adulterants—even in the amount of 10 per cent—it will not yield the metal, but will change to a whitish or yellowish matter. True naples yellow will yield tiny specks of metallic lead interspersed with a blackish metallic mass of antimony. The imitation naples yellow will not reduce in similar fashion.

Samples of naples yellow which I have tested, from pre-
sumably reputable firms, turned after burning to a yellowish mass representing the base and some coloring material.
Genuine cerulean blue and cobalt blue will not change their
color when burned. Cerulean blue, when boiled with nitric
acid, should leave a whitish residue of tin oxide that can be
reduced before the blow-pipe to metallic tin.

339. *Q. What are the chief adulterants for white lead and
zinc white?*

A. Barytes, whiting, clay. Zinc white will dissolve
completely in diluted nitric acid, hydrochloric acid, or aqua
regia. Effervescence or an undissolved residue will point to
the presence of a filler.

340. *Q. How can one test ultramarine? Viridian green?
Chrome oxide green? Manganese blue? Prussian blue?*

A. Ultramarine is not adulterated but there are inferior and better grades of the pigment. This paint, therefore, should be examined for purity and brilliance of tone,
rather than by chemical analysis, which would prove, on the
whole, inconclusive.

Viridian green and chrome oxide green dull may be
tested for the presence of a filler. (Q. 334.)

Manganese blue will turn green on boiling with washing soda. On treatment with acid, it will turn to purple.

Prussian blue when boiled with caustic turns to a
colorless or yellow solution with a red-brown precipitate.

341. *Q. How should one test the quality of earth colors?*

A. Because there is no standard quality for earth
colors—their composition changes with the locality in which
they are found—no conclusive chemical tests can be carried
out. Often one mine will contain pigments of differing quality. The best qualities of french or english ochres, cyprian
or turkish umber (the first comes from the island of Cyprus

in the Mediterranean, the latter from Asia Minor), terra di pozzuoli, burnt ochre (often referred to as light red), raw and burnt sienna should be compared with samples of unknown origin. As a rule, cheap materials will be impure and coarse. (It does not follow, however, that the expensive ones are always superior.) On the whole, domestic (American) earth colors are inferior in quality to the best foreign pigments.

When speaking of the quality of an ochre, for example, the following factors should be kept in mind; purity, composition, fineness of grain, and tinctorial properties. The pigment as it comes from the mine is purified by levigation; that is, by the washing and settling down of the pigment particles. The pigment, mixed with water, is channeled through a number of tanks, and the tank farthest from the outpour will contain the purest and finest grain of the pigment. But the composition of the pigment and its tinctorial properties will not be altered by this process.

342. *Q. What tests can be made to determine whether a cadmium color (cadmium yellow or red) is a pure cadmium-sulphide or a cadmium-barium pigment?*

A. Mix 1 part cadmium yellow with 4 parts hydrochloric acid. If the solution remains yellow, the pigment has been made with barium sulphate. If the solution becomes colorless, the pigment represents a cadmium sulphate. (Hydrogen sulphide gas will change the colorless solution back to the original color.)

343. *Q. How should one test zinc yellow?*

A. Boil zinc yellow with washing soda solution, filter or decant the yellow solution, wash, and repeat until the residue is colorless. Mix the residue with more dry washing soda or—better—anhydrous sodium carbonate, and test with blow-pipe (reduction to metallic zinc).

344. *Q. What test can be carried out to verify a genuine vermilion (sulphide of mercury)?*

A. When burned with the help of a blow-pipe, pure vermilion should evaporate, leaving no residue. Adulteration with carmine (cochineal) can be detected by placing the pigment, moistened with concentrated ammonia, on blotting paper. In the presence of a dye, a red stain will appear on the paper. A coal tar can be filtered through by washing the pigment with alcohol or benzene.

345. *Q. How can one test a vermilion color for the presence of mercury?*

A. A test for mercury can be carried out as follows: Heat vermilion strongly in a test tube, add powdered lamp black, or washing soda. Again expose to strong heat and watch for globules of mercury to appear at the sides of the tube. The tube should look silvery.

346. *Q. In order to test the pigment, how can one reduce an oil paint to dry pigment?*

A. Wash it repeatedly with benzene on a filter paper. When all of the oil is extracted, the dry pigment will remain.

347. *Q. How should a paint be tested for light fastness?*

A. Place the paint sample under glass, cover up part of it with tin foil, and expose to the sun for 600 hours; if at the end of this time it shows resistance to fading—comparison with the sample which was protected by the tin foil should be made—it is considered absolutely lightfast. (Commercial Standard—C.S. 2926.) This method, however, is not quite conclusive because the behavior of paint under the influence of direct sun rays is not always comparable to the behavior of paint under normal light conditions.

CHAPTER 14

Old Masters' Pigments

348. *Q. Which of the old masters' colors are still in use today?*

A. All the *earth colors,* such as ochres, red oxides, siennas, umbers, and green earth (terra verte). The lightest hue of the iron oxide was known as *terra di pozzuoli* or *terra rosa;* a pigment of a bright pink hue, it was found in the village of Pozzuoli in the environs of Naples. Not only the light red oxide, but also darker ones were—and still are —found in the same location. The darkest purple-red variety of the iron oxide was known as *caput mortuum,* a name which is now rarely used. (Our mars violet is of identical hue.) *Sinopia* was another name applied to the red oxides, although originally sinopia was a superior pigment mined in the city of Sinopia in Asia Minor, and sold under a seal as a Greek state monopoly.

The ochres and siennas varied, as they do today, in hue and opacity, depending on their source of origin; and so did *terra verte* (green earth). This latter color was used exclusively in tempera painting because an oil binder deprives it of opacity and its hue is too weak to be of any use as a glazing color. A particularly fine variety of *umber,* having a greenish cast, was found on the island of Cyprus and known as cyprian umber. It had a wider use than is generally assumed today. Pure brown color is not much in evidence in Renaissance painting—most of their brown colors, as seen today, are merely darkened varnishes and oils. Umber, however, did go into the mixture of a great many tones, such as grays, greens, and black. Moreover, umber was used as a standard siccative and as such was added to other colors and to oil grounds.

Other pigments which came to us from antiquity are: white lead, gypsum, naples yellow, minium, vermilion, bone black, and lamp black.

The principle of *white lead* manufactured by the "stack" or "Dutch" process is essentially the same today as it was ages ago. Coils of lead were put into clay pots containing vinegar, the lead and vinegar being placed in separate compartments. The pots were stacked together, covered up, and embedded in tan bark or dung. The lead was thus exposed to the fumes of acetic acid, carbon dioxide, heat, and moisture, which converted it into lead hydroxide and carbonate—our white lead. Washed and ground, the pigment was ready for use.

Other white pigments which cannot be used in connection with oil because of resulting loss of opacity, and yellowing are: marble dust, gypsum, egg shells ground to a fine pigment, and calcined fowl bones (one remembers Cennini's quaint advice—to collect these bones from under the table).

All these white pigments—excepting white lead— are quite useful when bound by a size for which white lead has no affinity. *Naples yellow* is a particularly valuable opaque yellow of ancient origin which can be considered absolutely permanent. It is said that naples yellow was first identified on enameled bricks found in ancient Babylon in 700 B.C. A manufactured pigment, it combines the oxide of lead and antimony; it is also reported that naples yellow was once found in natural state in Asia Minor.

Another ancient yellow is *massicot*. A lead oxide, it is prepared from white lead carefully heated. Its opacity equals that of white lead, and its siccative capacity is considerable.

Vermilion (cinnabar) is the most glorious of all the red pigments, and its history reaches back to ancient China. Although vermilion—a sulphide of mercury—has been, and still is, found in mercury veins, in early times it was also prepared synthetically. Its tonal variety ranges from bright orange to purple-red. Our present-day cadmium red, though identical in color, is finer in texture and does not possess the opacity of vermilion.

A very powerful orange-red, known as *minium,* is obtained by roasting lead. Today, it does not appear on the painter's palette, but it is still used in industry (under the name red lead), to protect structural steel before it receives a final coat of paint.

In the early periods, just as today, *black pigments* were produced by burning oil (lamp-black), charring bones (bone black), and charring shoots of grapevine (vine black). Other fine blacks were obtained by charring peach stones, almond shells, etc.

349. *Q. What were some of the other important colors of the past, superseded today by more permanent products?*

A. *Red colors*: Madder lake, brazil wood, cochineal. (Our modern equivalent for these colors is the analine dye alizarin crimson.) *Madder lake,* probably known as early as the fifteenth century, was derived from fermented roots of the madder plant. *Brazil wood* was extracted from brazil wood imported from India (the name brazil has no connection with the South American country) ; *cochineal* was obtained from dried bodies of the female insect *coccus cacti,* which lives in various cactus plants in Mexico and in Central and South America. All of these colors were dyes and had to be precipitated on a base of colorless pigments for use in oil painting. Their permanence was limited ; under favorable conditions, and when properly handled by the painter

—which was not always the case even during the time of the guilds—some of them did survive quite well. Besides these, there were various dyes of animal and vegetable origin, some of which have been used in watercolors and illuminated manuscripts.

A color exceedingly popular with the Renaissance painters was obtained from the mineral *malachite*. It is closely related to azurite and is often found in nature in a nearly pure state. Although fairly permanent when properly handled, it is no longer on the market.

Another copper color was *verdigris;* a copper acetate, it was obtained by corrosion of copper plates which were exposed to fermented grape skins.

Some of the yellow colors, such as *orpiment* (a sulphide of arsenic), were of mineral origin; others were organic compounds. Of this latter class was the *indian yellow* obtained in India from the dried urine of cows which were fed on mango tree leaves. (Present-day indian yellow is an analine color.) Weld (dyer's herb) was, among others, a source from which yellow paint was produced. Its color, as with all dyes, was precipitated on a base of finely pulverized egg shells, and remained transparent; or it was mixed with white lead, which resulted in an opaque yellow paint.

Finally, there were the blue colors, all of which are extinct today because of the superiority and cheapness of the modern blue colors. The ancient colors were: ultramarine, usually referred to as true ultramarine, which was obtained from the mineral *lapis lazuli* (lazurite). It was imported chiefly from Persia, and was perhaps the most expensive of all the colors. Depending on its purity, the blue was more or less intense; it was used mainly in tempera painting and less as an oil color. Present-day artificial ultramarine is chemically similar to the older color.

An especially fine Renaissance color, now obsolete, was *azurite blue* (azzurro della magna), a carbonate of copper found in many parts of Europe. When coarsely ground, this mineral yielded a darker hue of blue, and when finely ground, a lighter hue. Its value is particularly apparent in tempera techniques, where the blue appears lighter and more opaque.

I have been preparing azurite blue from a mineral found in San Juan County, Utah. The stones were first crushed in a bronze mortar, and the powder levigated in the usual manner, as follows: When shaken up with water, the coarse sand which the mineral contains settles down quickly, and the water which carries the pure pigment is poured off. The levigation was then repeated several times, and each time a finer sediment—now of pure color—was obtained. When the water evaporated, the various grades of pigments were separately washed with hot water to free them from soluble salts. When dry, the pigments were ready for use. This process of levigation is, however, quite tedious, so the early chemists devised several methods of pigment flotation. One of these calls for boiling the grind with soap; when the heavy sand settles down, the float containing the pure pigment is decanted.

An artificial copper color, almost as important as azurite and used during the time of the Renaissance, was the blue and green bice (*verditer*), an artificial basic copper carbonate (similar in color and chemical composition to azurite). And *smalt*, a finely ground glass colored to a deep blue by roasted cobalite, was another.

Another popular blue was *indigo,* a coloring matter extracted from certain plants in India and used mostly as a dye. As a precipitate, it was employed as an oil color. *Woad,* a plant native to Europe, also produced a color similar to indigo.

Numerous other inks and dyes were used chiefly industrially.

350. *Q. What colors were used in the time of ancient Rome?*

A. Earth colors such as: yellow ochre, red iron oxide, terra verte. Minerals: azurite, malachite, cinnabar (some of them were also artificially prepared). Manufactured colors: white lead, massicot (yellow oxide of lead), verdigris, orpiment. And the black colors: charcoal black, bone black, lamp black. Also various organic dyes.

351. *Q. How old are most of our modern colors?*

A. Prussian blue, discovered about 1704, came into use at the end of the 18th century. Cadmium yellow was commercially produced around 1850, and so was zinc white, although the latter was known long before that date. Artificial ultramarine was discovered in 1828, cobalt blue 25 years earlier; chrome oxide green and cerulean blue are each about 65 years old. The colors that have been introduced in our time are: phthalocyanine (monastral) blues and greens, manganese blue, barium yellow, titanium oxide, the mars colors, and the analine dyes—alizarin crimson and hansa yellow.

PART **2**

OIL PAINTING METHODS

CHAPTER 15

Toned Ground; Underpainting; Imprimatura

352. *Q. Beginning with the white canvas, what are the first steps?*

A. The transfer of the drawing to the canvas (unless of course, the drawing was done directly upon the canvas).

353. *Q. How does one transfer a drawing?*

A. The drawing, executed on paper, should be transferred by means of a transfer paper. This paper may be prepared by rubbing some iron oxide pigment or umber (or a pastel crayon) into a thin detail paper. Commercially produced graphite transfer paper can also be used. However, a carbon transfer paper should be avoided, for the carbon color will bleed through (strike through) a subsequent paint layer. The actual tracing is carried out by placing the paper face down on the canvas, next going over the drawing's contours with a pencil or a pointed instrument.

354. *Q. With the drawing transferred and fixed with a fixative, what is the next move?*

A. Two principal methods can be employed: The first is suitable for smooth surfaces (such as found on a gesso panel), the second on canvas. Let us start with the first, called imprimatura.

IMPRIMATURA

355. *Q. What is an imprimatura and what is its purpose?*

A. Imprimatura and glaze are identical conditions of

101

a paint film. Specifically, imprimatura refers to the stain-
ing of a painting ground with a thin film of a transparent
color—a step in preparation of the ground. Imprimatura
serves to cover up the white color of the painting ground,
or to modify or change the tonality of a toned ground or an
underpainting.

356. *Q. When is the use of imprimatura especially recommended?*

A. On small, smooth canvases for quick, sketchy techniques which permit some of the imprimatura color to remain uncovered on tiny areas. When heavy overpaintings
are contemplated, the use of imprimatura serves no purpose.

357. *Q. What colors can be used for imprimatura?*

A. For painting flesh tones, a stain of burnt sienna
is quite appropriate when a bright color is desired. For
grays or greens, burnt sienna and viridian green can be used
or viridian green and umber. All the transparent colors, as
well as the opaque, will do well for imprimatura if diluted
with the medium to watercolor consistency.

358. *Q. What thinning medium should be used for imprimatura?*

A. Oil paint of normal consistency should be diluted
with a copal varnish. (For copal varnish, *see* Q. 179.)

359. *Q. How should one apply imprimatura to a canvas or
panel ground?*

A. The paint may be brushed in with a stiff brush
and then, if desired, partially wiped off with a rag; or it can
rubbed in with the palm of the hand in similar fashion as in
inking an etched plate.

360. *Q. How long does it take for the imprimatura to dry?*

A. Because of the volatile medium, imprimatura will
become dry in less than half an hour. However, one should

wait a few days to allow the imprimatura to solidify and to become resistant to the action of the turpentine which our painting medium contains. (For painting medium, *see* Q. 212.)

TONED GROUND

361. *Q. What is a toned ground and what is its purpose?*

A. An opaque ground of uniformly solid color applied on top of the white lead priming is referred to as a toned ground. It facilitates the progress of the painting because it does away with the original white color of the ground.

362. *Q. What colors should be used for a toned ground?*

A. As a rule, light pastel shades are best. As in all underpainting (Q. 368), white lead should be the chief constituent of the paint. For a yellowish tone, ochre should be added to white; and for a pink tone, venetian red. A gray ground can be prepared with white lead, umber, and prussian blue. Such a ground will be most suitable for painting portraits. Also, a solid red ground may be used; red grounds were greatly favored by the Venetian painters of the 16th to 18th centuries.

363. *Q. What painting medium should be used in preparing a toned ground?*

A. The paint should be stiff and lean. No more oil medium should be used than is required to obtain a paint of normal (i.e. brushable) consistency. A paint that is too stiff can be somewhat thinned with the Copal Painting Medium.

364. *Q. What tools should be used for applying a toned ground?*

A. A not too flexible, large palette knife is best. Such a knife will force the paint into the interstices of the canvas and produce the thinnest film possible.

UNDERPAINTING

365. *Q. What is underpainting?*

A. Underpainting is a modified toned ground in that different colors are applied to different areas.

366. *Q. What is the value of underpainting?*

A. To create textures; to facilitate glazing and scumbling; to influence the coloristic appearance of a painting.

367. *Q. What painting medium should be used in underpainting?*

A. Use no medium at all; if the paint is too stiff, dilute it a little with Copal Painting Medium.

368. *Q. What colors should be used in underpainting?*

A. As a rule, all colors should be intermixed with white lead to create a solid foundation.

369. *Q. Can one use an imprimatura on top of an underpainting?*

A. To increase the intensity of colors in the underpainting an imprimatura of pure cadmium yellow, red, etc., can be brushed on top of the underpainting.

370. *Q. What tools should be used in executing an underpainting?*

A. A stiff paint can best be distributed with a palette knife. When a brush is used, harsh marks should be subdued with a blender.

371. *Q. How long should an underpainting dry before painting on it?*

A. A thin paint film consisting chiefly of white lead, prussian blue, and umber will be sufficiently dry in a few days. Thicker paint layers, and layers consisting of slower drying colors, may need from two weeks to one month or longer to dry well.

372. *Q. Can one safely use siccative in underpainting to accelerate the drying?*

A. In an amount of 1/10 of 1 per cent to 1/5 of 1 per cent of the weight of the paint, the use of siccative is not detrimental. (For siccative, *see* Q. 157-165.)

373. *Q. Have all painters, at all times, used underpainting?*

A. Until about the middle of the 19th century the artists, as a rule, used underpainting, or at least an imprimatura. The Impressionists did not use it methodically. Cézanne did not use it. Today there is again a tendency to utilize underpainting systematically and purposefully.

374. *Q. What is grisaille?*

A. Underpainting in gray colors, chiefly used for underpainting flesh in portraits, for figure painting, and for draperies. (*See* Q. 379.)

375. *Q. What are the advantages of painting in grisaille?*

A. In portrait painting, form and likeness can be well modeled and repeatedly corrected without muddying a painting by frequent overpainting with colors. Grisaille, because it is made up chiefly of white lead with some other color added, is the most solid and lean foundation, safeguarding a painting's permanence. Grisaille is also most suitable for glazing because of its dense body and light color.

376. *Q. Of what colors should the grisaille be made?*

A. White lead may be tinted with umber and prussian blue, or umber and ultramarine. Silvery gray, bluish, brownish, or neutral gray tints can be obtained with these colors. A yellowish or greenish tint can be produced by an addition of ochre, and pink tones by admixture of venetian red.

377. *Q. Why is black color not very suitable for mixing gray tints?*

A. The tonal range of grays produced from black is limited. Moreover, black color retards the drying of paints.

378. *Q. What medium should one use for grisaille?*

A. No medium at all; when the paint is too stiff to be moved freely, it may be loosened up with some Copal Painting Medium.

379. *Q. Where do we find grisaille in the old masters' paintings?*

A. Grisaille was mostly used in flesh and also in garments which were to be glazed with madder lake, ultramarine, azurite blue, the copper greens, etc. Often other objects such as rocks, water, etc., received a grisaille underpainting.

380. *Q. Should one oil the underpainting before starting to paint?*

A. In order to reduce friction between the brush and the painted surface, as well as to increase the luminosity of colors, oiling should be carried out.

381. *Q. How should one oil an underpainting?*

A. A little of the Copal Painting Medium should be rubbed into the underpainting with a stiff brush or one's finger. (On small areas this finger method is especially practical.) Any surplus oil should be removed with a lint-free cloth or an elastic and rather sharp-edged palette knife; a stiff dull knife would be entirely unsuitable. Only the thinnest film of the painting medium should remain on the surface.

CHAPTER 16

Painting; Glazing; Scumbling

382. *Q. What is painting "alla prima"?*

A. Strictly speaking, the term refers to finishing a painting in one session while painting wet in wet without the use of underpainting.

383. *Q. What are the advantages of using a resinous medium?*

A. Overpaintings may be carried out with little delay, since two fresh paint layers executed with a resinous medium will combine and eventually dry out as one. (Oil medium alone does not have the capacity to soften an underlying paint film.)

384. *Q. How can one produce a paint surface with maximum gloss?*

A. The more thoroughly polymerized oil medium—see Question 124—(with or without varnish) will produce greater gloss. However, in order to obtain high gloss, one must paint on a largely nonabsorbent and completely dry surface. A surface which is not dry—that is, a surface which has not sufficiently solidified—will absorb oil from the top paint layer. Such painting will dry out flat. Oiling of surface preceding painting is imperative in order to produce a glossy effect. As a rule, paint which dries quickly will retain more gloss; especially when siccative is used the gloss will be quite pronounced. Slow drying colors, on the other hand, have the tendency to dry out flat.

385. *Q. Is a glossy paint surface desirable?*

A. Dirt will not cling easily to such a surface. Moreover, the depth of the color is enhanced by gloss. Gloss also indicates that the pigments are bound with a sufficient quantity of oil, hence maximum elasticity of paint film is insured. (On the other hand, an excess of polymerized oil can be responsible for enamel-like surfaces which may reflect light unpleasantly.)

386. *Q. How can one obtain a flat (mat) paint surface?*

A. Mat surface may be produced by: (1) painting on absorbent ground; (2) presence of turpentine in the medium (in absence of resin) ; (3) the use of paint as it comes from the tube without additional oil medium. A glossy, dry paint film if carefully rubbed with a turpentine-moistened rag will attain a mat appearance. All these measures, however, are detrimental to the permanence of the painting.

387. *Q. How should one best apply one paint layer on top of another?*

A. Brush marks and all impasto which may become disturbing when overpainted should be scraped off with a scraper or flattened with sandpaper. Before this can be done, the paint film must be dry throughout.

388. *Q. What is trickling of the overpainting and how can one prevent it?*

A. When a paint or the painting medium does not spread to cover a surface uniformly but contracts, staying on it in little drops (like water on a highly polished surface), this behavior is called trickling. In order to make the surface receptive to the next paint application, some turpentine should be brushed on it and allowed to evaporate.

389. *Q. How many overpaintings can be carried out?*

A. Providing that all the rules governing permanent

painting are observed, there is, theoretically speaking, no limit to the number of paint layers which may follow one another.

390. *Q. Which is the best method of removing a paint film?*

A. A fresh paint film or a glaze can be removed with mineral spirits or turpentine. A hardened paint layer may be rubbed down with sandpaper. It can also be dissolved with a mixture of benzene and toluene, or acetone.

391. *Q. In oil painting, is it advisable to start with darker or with lighter values?*

A. When following traditional techniques, one will start with the darker values while painting wet in wet. Since heightening of light values requires the use of larger quantities of white color, this procedure is logical. Should one start loading the painting with white color from the beginning, muddy or chalky tones will result.

392. *Q. Is it advisable to paint in colors contrasting with the color of the underpainting, or should the two color schemes be related to each other?*

A. It all depends on the artist's individual preference. Generally, the final color should be in contrast to the underlying colors, because contrasting colors, when superimposed, will enhance one another. On the other hand, superimposition of identical colors can render them dull. It is also advantageous to overpaint a warm color with a cold color, and vice versa.

GLAZING

393. *Q. What is a glaze?*

A. An application of a transparent color which is darker in hue than the underlying color.

394. *Q. When was the glazing technique developed?*

A. The first paintings revealing expert use of transparent colors on underpainting prepared especially for this purpose date from about 1400. This does not imply that the use of transparent oil colors was not known centuries or even thousands of years before this date, but no examples of great easel paintings have reached us from times before the Renaissance.

395. *Q. Where was the glazing technique developed?*

A. It is generally accepted that the technique was perfected by Jan van Eyck in Flanders and then introduced into Italy and other European countries.

396. *Q. Which are the glazing colors?*

A. Any color may be used for glazing when sufficiently diluted with the medium to make it transparent. However, some colors are by nature transparent—that is, when compounded with a normal quantity of the vehicle. These glazing colors are: alizarin crimson, ultramarine blue, prussian blue, manganese blue, viridian green, mars orange, barium yellow, hansa yellow, indian yellow, raw and burnt sienna, monastral blue and green, green earth, gold ochre.

397. *Q. What medium is best for use in glazing?*

A. Glazing medium should be composed of oil and varnish. Heat-processed oils—that is, sun-thickened oil or standoil—are preferable to the unpolymerized linseed oil. Varnish is needed to make a limpid application adhere to the surface and to reduce the oil content of the medium which, in glazes, is usually excessively high.

398. *Q. Which resin is more suitable for glazing, damar or copal?*

A. Because of its resistance to deterioration, a medium compounded with copal is preferable. Damar resin should not be used as part of the painting medium if permanence is desired.

399. *Q. How soon should a painting be glazed?*

A. When a finished painting is to be glazed (its color modified by a transparent color film), early application is advisable in order to make the glaze become an integral part of the paint stratum. A thinly executed painting can be glazed as soon as it is superficially dry—that is, in a few days. A thicker film will solidify in a week or more.

400. *Q. What types of glazing can be used?*

A. Either a glaze executed on a finished painting which has dried, or a glaze executed on the underpainting during the process of painting. The first procedure serves to modify—intensify or subdue—a color, or to achieve a coloristic effect which cannot be obtained by other means. A glaze may also be put into a wet color film. This, however, can be done more easily with a palette knife than with a brush.

401. *Q. How should a glaze be executed?*

A. A surface which is to receive a glaze should first be moistened with the medium. The color may then be applied with a brush—any type—or with a palette knife, or it may be rubbed in with a finger or with the palm of the hand (as when inking an etching plate).

402. *Q. How many glazes can be applied?*

A. One or two glazes are all that can be used, because the film would no longer be transparent if it were composed of several paint applications.

403. *Q. Can one overpaint a glaze safely with an opaque color?*

A. From the viewpoint of performance, because it contains too much oil, it is best to remove a glaze before continuing to paint. This can be done with mineral spirits, or a fine sandpaper. In case the underpainting has been damaged or has become discolored, a new foundation should be prepared.

404. *Q. Should there be considerable difference between the hue of the underpainting and the glaze?*

A. The greater the difference, the more luminous the glaze will appear; the light color of the underpainting will also obviate future darkening and yellowing of the glaze.

405. *Q. Are glazings permanent? Are they liable to deteriorate in time?*

A. Thin glazes are susceptible to injury when cleaning and revarnishing paintings. (Q. 389, 419.) Glazes tend to become more transparent with the passage of time.

SCUMBLING

406. *Q. What is a scumble?*

A. An application of a light, semi-transparent color on top of a darker underpainting. The process of applying the scumble is called scumbling.

407. *Q. Which colors are useful for scumbling?*

A. White, and all the lighter colors; also dark colors when mixed with white. All colors, however, must be applied thinly.

408. *Q. How should one execute a scumble?*

A. One may either paint on a dried surface or paint wet in wet. It is advisable to oil a dried surface before scumbling.

409. *Q. Are scumbles permanent?*

A. As a rule, scumbles are liable to go down in tone with age.

VARIOUS TINTS

410. *Q. Which colors will produce realistic flesh tints?*

A. The principal ones are white, ultramarine, light ochre, umber.

411. *Q. How can one obtain gray tints?*

A. Mixture of one of the blue colors with umber and white will produce various cold and warm grays, as will a mixture of viridian green, umber, and white; red and green and white; and black and white.

412. *Q. How can one obtain pink tints?*

A. By mixing any of the red iron oxides, or cadmium red, or vermilion, or burnt sienna, in mixtures with white or naples yellow. The dark iron oxides will tend to turn violetish in the presence of white; ochre may reduce such tones to pink.

413. *Q. How can one mix violet tints?*

A. Venetian red, cadmium red, vermilion, or alizarin crimson mixed with ultramarine (and white) will yield a variety of violet hues.

414. *Q. How can one obtain green tints?*

A. All the blue colors and black when mixed with yellow colors will give green tints.

415. *Q. Can one produce yellow, blue, and red tints?*

A. These colors are basic, or primary, and cannot be obtained from mixtures of other colors.

CHAPTER 17

Cleaning; Repairing

416. *Q. How can one remove dust or lint which may have gathered on a wet painting?*

A. Paintings soiled in this manner should first be permitted to dry thoroughly. Then, by rubbing the paint surface with one's finger, foreign matter can, as a rule, be removed. Should the impurities be firmly embedded in the paint film, careful polishing with pulverized pumice stone mixed with oil may be required. Often retouching of the damaged surface may be necessary.

417. *Q. How should a relatively fresh painting be cleaned?*

A. After dusting off with a soft cloth, the paint surface may be rubbed with a piece of bread kneaded to resemble a gum eraser. Another efficient method of removing superficial dirt is to rub the surface with one's finger. (As everyone knows, dirt easily attaches itself to one's hands.)

418. *Q. How should one remove varnish and dirt embedded in it from a relatively fresh painting?*

A. A Picture Cleaning Medium of my own formulation prepared from mineral spirits and xylene and manufactured by Permanent Pigments of Cincinnati, Ohio, is an efficient agent for this purpose.

419. *Q. Should one use a solvent to clean glazed parts of a painting?*

A. Fresh glazes executed with a resinous medium are susceptible to injury by even a mild solvent; therefore, greatest care should be exerted, and hard or prolonged rubbing must be avoided.

420. *Q. How should one remove dirt embedded in a heavy impasto?*

A. A stiff bristle brush moistened with an appropriate solvent is best for cleaning dirt from the crevices.

421. *Q. Should strong solvents be used in stubborn cases?*

A. On paintings of recent date strong solvents such as benzene, toluene, xylene, acetone, etc., should not be used undiluted. They can injure a paint film and will easily destroy glazes.

422. *Q. Are old paintings also likely to be injured by a strong solvent?*

A. Regardless of their age, paint films executed with a medium containing excessive amounts of resin, damar, and mastic remain susceptible to the action of all resin solvents. Therefore, before using a strong solvent on an old painting ("old" in the sense of "antique") the nature and condition of the paint film should be determined. Such an examination may best be carried out on the edge of the painting. One must also ascertain what kind of film obstructs or dims an old painting. Such a film may be made up of old and yellowed varnish (oil-resin varnish, for example) or of dirt which has become incorporated into the paint film. A darkened and yellowed paint film may itself be taken for a surface film. In this instance cleaning will not be a proper remedy, but exposure to strong light may ameliorate the condition.

423. *Q. How should an oil or oil-varnish film be removed from antique paintings?*

A. Copaiba balsam mixed with turpentine in equal parts can be applied to the paint surface and left on for a period of 24 hours or longer. Through this procedure, the underlying oil or oil-varnish film can be softened and thus made more susceptible to the action of a strong solvent, such as xylene, benzene, toluene, or acetone. Wood alcohol (methyl alcohol) is another powerful solvent for both varnish and oil films. Of course greatest care should be observed when using these powerful solvents. When cleaning a painting with alcohol, turpentine is usually employed as a "restrainer"; that is, if used immediately after the application of alcohol, it stops its action. When mixed with alcohol, turpentine also reduces its "bite." Another powerful agent is saponine. The white powder should be mixed with water so that it foams, and some ammonia should be added to strengthen its action.

424. *Q. Should soap and water be used to clean paintings?*

A. If the canvas does not carry a gesso priming, moistening a fresh painting with water will not necessarily harm it. If gesso priming is present and moisture penetrates the oil film and permeates the canvas, the painting will suffer. Because it is not in the nature of gesso to follow the expansion and contraction of the wet canvas, cracking of the ground and the paint itself will follow. As far as the soap is concerned, it would be quite difficult to remove it from the crevices of a paint impasto, and even a mild soap might prove injurious to a paint film. A moist canvas can cause cracking of an aged paint film, even though it does not rest on a gesso foundation. This is especially true where the canvas support is stronger than the paint film.

425. *Q. Can a yellowed and darkened painting be improved?*

A. This depends on the cause of the condition. Yellowing due to storage of a painting in darkness can be improved by exposure for a period of several weeks to a strong light, or a mild reflected sunlight. However, if yellowing and darkening of a painting have occurred as a result of improper technique or faulty materials (improper formulation of paint, inferior oils, pigments, faulty painting ground), the discoloration of the painting cannot be remedied.

RESTORING

426. *Q. What is a "bloom"?*

A. A bluish veil sometimes observed on paintings and especially noticeable on the dark areas.

427. *Q. What are the causes of bloom, and what is the remedy?*

A. It is assumed that moisture condensation underneath the varnish film is responsible for this disturbing effect, which explains why varnishing on a rainy day is inadvisable. Mastic varnish is apt to cause bloom on a painting when applied under adverse conditions. On the other hand, paintings varnished with damar rarely show the presence of bloom. Old paintings with a defective support (rotten canvas, for example) are especially liable to be affected. Sometimes, rubbing of the varnish surface with a chamois or a silk cloth may improve the condition. More often, however, the removal of the varnish and revarnishing is indicated. Old paintings which develop bloom repeatedly will have to be relined. (*See* Q. 441) Generally this helps to inhibit development of bloom.

428. *Q. How can one flatten out bulges and creases on canvas caused by pressure of an object against it, or by stretchers or crossbars?*

A. Slight moistening of the damaged area on the reverse side of the canvas is recommended while the paint-

ing is still fresh—that is, not older than a few years—and
if the canvas does not carry a gesso ground. If these factors
are not considered, cracking of the paint may result. When
the canvas is moistened, the keys of the stretcher should
be tightened. In severe cases, the moist canvas areas should
be flattened with a moderately warm flatiron, but some
cracks may remain visible after the treatment.

429. *Q. How can one flatten out bulges on older paintings
or on a broken gesso ground, and smooth out cracked
areas?*

A. Relatively minor defects can be often remedied
as follows: (1) Place the canvas flat on a table with the
painted surface downward; where the crack or bulge appears, place several sheets of newspaper on the table to
serve as a cushion. (2) Cut a piece of blotting paper about
one inch larger all around than the damaged surface of
the painting; moisten the blotting paper slightly with
water and place it on the back of the canvas. (3) Insert
newspaper sheets all around the edge of the blotting paper
(in order to prevent its impression on the canvas). (4)
Cover the blotting paper with several sheets of newspaper
and weight it down with a heavy laundry iron. (Newspaper
sheets should be replaced as soon as they have absorbed
the moisture from the blotting paper.) The weight should
remain on the canvas for at least 24 hours.

430. *Q. Should one overpaint a cracked area?*

A. Only minor and superficial cracks such as do not
involve the ground—or a heavy impasto—can be successfully overpainted...

431. *Q. How should one fill deep scratches and holes in a
painting executed on a panel?*

A. A gesso, such as used for priming a panel, should
be used. Sufficient amounts of whiting should be added to

make a stiff paste, and 20 per cent of a thick damar solution (Q. 181) should be emulsified with the gesso by means of a palette knife. The palette knife will also serve to fill all the holes and crevices on the panel with the gesso-resin emulsion. Often it is advisable to add a dry pigment (instead of the whiting) to the gesso emulsion in order to approximate the color of the surrounding areas.

432. *Q. How should one prepare a putty to fill holes in a paint film resting on a canvas?*

A. If the support (the fiber of the canvas) is also uncovered, some glue size should be applied to it with a small brush. Upon drying, the hole should be filled by means of a palette knife, using a putty prepared from a stiff white lead paint mixed with copal varnish and umber. The latter acts as a dryer, and its color provides a neutral underpainting. Shallow holes may be filled with one application. Deeper crevices should receive a few successive layers of the putty; each one should dry well before the next application.

433. *Q. How can one repair a small tear in a canvas?*

A. By attaching a transparent Scotch tape over the tear, on the reverse side of the painting. (For treatment of larger damages, *see* "relining," Q. 437.)

434. *Q. How should one repair a hole in a canvas?*

A. A round patch of thin linen (thinner than the original canvas in order to avoid its making an impression on the paint surface) should be frayed and made fuzzy around the edges with a piece of sandpaper. For an adhesive, use equal quantities of damar or mastic resin and beeswax. These ingredients should be fused together (by heating them in a spoon, for example). A small addition of venice turpentine will increase the adhesive power of the compound.

435. *Q. Why should one not use glue as an adhesive?*

A. A patch which is affixed to a canvas by means of glue will invariably cause the canvas to pull all around the patch, making wrinkles.

436. *Q. How should a patch be applied?*

A. After covering with the adhesive the area of the patch to be attached to the canvas—also the space around the damaged canvas—press the patch onto the canvas with a moderately warm laundry iron. When left undisturbed, the patch will adhere to the canvas indefinitely. Before overpainting, any surplus adhesive should be thoroughly removed, and the surface equalized.

437. *Q. How should one treat damages which cannot be repaired in the manner just described?*

A. In many cases relining will help—that is, mounting the old canvas on a new one, or on a panel.

438. *Q. What support should be chosen for relining?*

A. (1) Raw canvas, (2) Masonite, (3) prepared painter's canvas carrying an oil ground. For the inexperienced, the use of a Masonite panel is the easiest.

439. *Q. What adhesive should be used to cement two canvases together?*

A. There are two general types of adhesives—one is aqueous; the other, nonaqueous. The standard formulas are: (1) Wallpaper paste, 1 ounce dissolved in 4 ounces of water; glue, 2 ounces (glue should be soaked in water overnight, then dissolved in the other ingredients); finally venice turpentine, ½ ounce, is added to and emulsified in the hot wallpaper paste-glue solution. (2) White lead oil paint of stiff consistency mixed with venice turpentine to a brushable paste. (3) Flour paste, 1 part, mixed with venice turpentine. (4) Beeswax, 1 part, melted with damar resin,

1 part, and venice turpentine, 10 per cent. (*See also* Q. 440.)
(5) Casein latex cement. It is of relatively recent origin,
and the one easiest to handle by a nonprofessional restorer.
This medium (also known as polymer emulsion) is my own
preference. It should be applied to the rough side of the
Masonite, as well as to the canvas. The whole should be
covered up with a piece of Masonite and weighed down with
a cinder block for a period of 24 hours.

440. *Q. Is there hazard in using an aqueous adhesive?*

A. Some canvases (paintings) may shrink considerably when wetting of the entire surface is carried out. A
canvas 25-inches long may shrink as much as ½ inch, sometimes more. Also the grain of the canvas can become dis-
turbingly pronounced.

441. *Q. What is the procedure in relining a painting?*

A. When a raw (extra strong) canvas or a prepared
canvas is used, it must first be stretched on an extra heavy
stretcher and then sized. (The ordinary commercial stretchers may be too weak to stand the pull.) The stretched canvas should be several inches larger all around than the canvas to be relined. Next, the painting is taken off the old
stretcher, cut at the edge where the canvas folds around the
stretcher, and its back thoroughly sandpapered in order to
remove all the irregularities and roughness of the fabric.
Then the back of the painting and the face of the new canvas should be covered with the chosen adhesive, after which
the two are pressed tightly together. Care should be taken
to attach the canvas evenly by first pressing it with a rub-
ber roller (or with the palm of the hand) and then, when
the adhesive has set, the hole should be ironed with an
extra heavy warm laundry iron. This ironing should be carried out on the back of the new canvas and not on the surface of the picture. Finally, the relined painting should be
taken off its preliminary stretchers and placed between ply-

wood or Masonite panels (protected by layers of tissue paper) and pressed together by means of carpenter clamps. in arranging the clamps, stiff strips of wood should be placed at the sides of the panel in order to permit the clamps to exert even pressure all over the painting. The painting should be removed from the press after several days and placed on its permanent stretchers without delay; otherwise the remaining moisture will make it curl. The stretchers used for this purpose should be of a heavy type.

442. *Q. What should be the chief consideration when ironing the canvas, or applying any kind of heavy pressure (such as the powerful clamp presses) to it?*

A. Avoidance of too heavy pressure which might easily flatten out all impasto on a fresh painting. Even older paintings can suffer a flattening of paint configuration when heavy pressure is applied. Especially when an aqueous adhesive has been used, a relatively fresh painting may not only shrink but emerge from the operation looking like a flat color print.

443. *Q. How should one proceed when using wax-resin adhesive?*

A. Resin and wax should be melted over an electric heater; venice turpentine (which has also been heated to allow free flowing) is then added, and well mixed with the resin and wax (*see* Q. 439, part 4). The prepared side of the new canvas (meaning the side which carries the oil ground), and also the back of the painting, are then generously covered with the adhesive by means of a palette knife, after which the two are pressed together. Ironing with a warm electric iron should follow.

444. *Q. What conditions are detrimental to the permanence of oil paintings?*

A. Humidity and excessive changes of temperature.

Canvas, as well as some wood panels, contract or expand excessively under these conditions and this leads to cracking of the paint film. Steam heat especially, which accounts for abnormally dry air, may cause even a well-constructed wood panel to crack.

445. *Q. What are other causes of cracking, and what types of cracks may develop on a paint surface?*

A. Cracks may be found on the paint surface only, or they can involve the ground as well. In the first instance, overpainting can cover up a crack, providing the paint film involved is quite thin. In the second, overpainting eventually will crack too. The causes of cracks are: (1) Damage from pressure against a canvas; these are irregular, sharp cracks involving the painting as well as the ground. (2) Excess of glue in gesso or size—such cracks are known as "glue-worms," which best describes their appearance. The only remedy here is relining under pressure. (3) Rolling of canvas carrying a heavy impasto will cause long, horizontal, sharp cracks. (Relining will minimize the effect.) (4) Forceful keying of stretchers—long diagonal cracks, often covering the entire canvas. Also, when restretching a canvas carrying gesso ground, cracks may develop close to the edge of the stretchers when canvas is forcefully pulled. Here, too, relining is the only remedy. (5) A net of fine, web-like cracks seen on old paintings—and referred to as "crackle"—is caused by the incapacity of a brittle paint film to follow the expansion and contraction of the canvas. (6) So-called alligator cracks (like a design on an alligator skin) are caused by painting on an underpainting which has not sufficiently dried; or by superimposition of paint layers which vary greatly in drying capacity, as well as in oil content—in other words, when painting with a lean vehicle on an oil-saturated underpainting. Such cracks are shallow and develop shortly after a painting has been executed. When the paint film dries out thoroughly, no further action takes place and the cracks can then be filled in and overpainted. (7) Circular cracks, found particularly on some paintings from the late 18th and early 19th centuries, are said to result from oversmooth grounds. Some authorities attribute this condition to storage of paintings in very cold rooms. It would seem, however, that the quality of the support and the manner of priming during those periods might be responsible for this occurrence. (8) Painting on entirely nonabsorbent smooth grounds may also produce cracks. These are wide as well as hair-fine fissures which clearly reveal the underlying ground. (9) Improper formulation of paint can cause a variety of cracks, mostly of the alligator type. This danger does not exist when using present-day, reliable paints. It was, however, quite common with many of the European paints manufactured during the 19th century and the beginnings of the 20th century. Excessive use of wax, water, or other materials as stabilizers was responsible for various types of cracks. (10) Certain obsolete paints, such as vandyke brown (asphaltum) and others, will, as a rule, produce fissures of the alligator type whether applied straight or in mixtures with other paints. (11) Excessive use of dryers, and the use of improper dryers, such as lead, manganese, etc., will cause cracking of the paint.

PART **3**

TEMPERA PAINTING

CHAPTER 18

Egg-Tempera Painting

446. *Q. What is tempera painting?*

A. A type of painting in which the dry pigments are mixed with an emulsion possessing such properties that the paint may be diluted with water or with oil.

447. *Q. What emulsions have such properties?*

A. Emulsions of egg, oil, and water; or varnish, gum arabic (glue, etc.), and water; or oil, gum arabic, and water; or oil, varnish, egg (or gum arabic, glue, etc.), and water.

448. *Q. What is an emulsion? What is the best-known emulsion for tempera painting?*

A. Briefly, an emulsion is a suspension of fine particles or globules of a liquid in a liquid. In paintmaking, an emulsion is normally a suspension of oleaginous or resinous material in an aqueous liquid (or of an aqueous liquid in an oil), with egg, casein, glue, or gum. Egg yolk, long known in the field of tempera painting, is one of the most nearly perfect and best-known natural emulsions. Painting using egg yolk as a medium is known as egg-tempera painting.

449. *Q. What are the properties of egg yolk?*

A. Egg yolk consists of water, fat, lecithin, protein, dextrose, cholesterol, lutein, and other substances. Upon drying, the yolk becomes waterproof and develops great elasticity and toughness. It does not yellow, crack, or darken. (For egg white, *see* Q. 474.)

450. *Q. How is the egg medium combined with pigments?*

A. The egg yolk is separated from the white, then the thin skin which encloses the yolk, and all the small threads of mucilage are pinched off. If used undiluted, the yolk would be too greasy; therefore, the yolk of one egg should receive an addition of 2 to 4 teaspoonfuls of water. In order to preserve the mixture from decomposing, 3 drops of vinegar may be mixed with the yolk and water. This medium is then combined with the pigments, which have previously been ground to a paste in water with a muller. (These paste-colors, if placed in screw-cap jars, will last indefinitely.)

451. *Q. How should one mix the paste pigment with the egg medium?*

A. About equal parts of the pigment and medium are placed on a palette (or in a cup) and mixed thoroughly with a stiff brush or a palette knife. A correctly tempered paint should dry with a slight gloss.

452. *Q. What consistency should the paints possess?*

A. They should be as thin and limpid as thin oil colors.

453. *Q. How can one ascertain that a pigment has received a sufficient amount of the tempera binder (medium)?*

A. A sample of the paint is applied to glass. After 24 hours it should be possible to scrape the solidified film off. If the film crumbles, this will indicate that not enough binder has been compounded with the paint. Once one has the right relationship between the amounts of pigment and binder, as much water as necessary for brushability can be added.

454. *Q. Should one prepare the paint for prolonged use?*

A. It is best to prepare the paint for a day's use

only. However, as we have seen, a few drops of vinegar will keep the egg yolk from decomposing.

455. *Q. Why do some egg-tempera paintings appear much lighter after drying?*

A. The pigments have not received enough of the binder.

456. *Q. Why do some egg-tempera paintings turn spotty and dark after varnishing?* (For varnishing, *see* Q. 188-193.)

A. For the same reason—insufficient egg medium.

457. *Q. Why do some egg-tempera paintings appear too shiny after drying?*

A. The paint has been prepared with too much egg yolk.

458. *Q. Why do some paints dry out quickly and some slowly?*

A. Rapid drying indicates lack of the binder; slow drying suggests excess of egg medium. Also, a thick paint film will dry out more slowly.

459. *Q. What support and what kind of priming should be used for egg-tempera painting?*

A. Gesso panels offer the best support. (*See* Q. 58-64.)

460. *Q. How can one make certain that the gesso has been correctly prepared?*

A. Tempera paint should acquire a slight gloss, when dry and polished with a soft material. When a painting remains flat (dull), it indicates that the ground is too absorbent.

461. *Q. What is the general procedure in handling the brush in egg-tempera technique?*

A. Since blending of colors in the fashion of oil painting cannot very well be carried out, brushes are used for hatching and cross-hatching to produce tonal transition. Round sable brushes are best suited for such a technique. However, the aims of a painter will ultimately decide what kind of a tool he should use.

462. *Q. Should one treat egg-tempera in an opaque or a transparent fashion?*

A. This technique lends itself best to semitransparent applications.

463. *Q. Can one underpaint with egg tempera in monotones?*

A. Monotones of a light color are most suitable for underpainting.

464. *Q. How often can one overpaint an egg-tempera painting?*

A. As often as one needs in order to achieve a desired effect. There is no reason to wait until the underpainting solidifies before commencing with the overpainting.

465. *Q. Should one paint dark on light, or light on dark?*

A. Because the paint is semitransparent, it is logical to keep the underpainting in light colors.

466. *Q. Must the overpainting always be in egg tempera?*

A. No. One can paint very well with oil paints on an underpainting executed in pure egg yolk color.

467. *Q. Is any means taken to protect egg-tempera paintings once they are completed?*

A. Yes. Often they are varnished.

468. *Q. What kind of varnish is used?*

A. The same as for oil painting (*see* Q. 181, 182).

469. *Q. Does tempera painting change in color when varnished?*

A. Only paint which has not enough binder will change, appearing much darker after the application of varnish.

470. *Q. How soon should a tempera painting be varnished?*

A. Unlike oil paintings, egg-tempera paintings may be varnished shortly after their completion, that is, in one or several weeks, depending on the thickness of the paint stratum.

471. *Q. Is it advisable to protect the varnished painting with wax?*

A. Yes. Wax offers added protection. (For waxing, *see* Q. 195, 196. It is especially easy to wax a panel.)

472. *Q. Does tempera painting—like work in oil—darken when kept in darkness?*

A. Darkness has no influence on paint which is not compounded with oil.

473. *Q. Are egg-tempera paints permanent?*

A. They are more permanent than paints mixed with any other binder.

474. *Q. Is egg white alone ever used in tempera painting?*

A. Very seldom. The pure yolk, free from white, is generally preferred.

475. *Q. What are the constituents, properties, and uses of the white of egg in painting?*

A. Egg white consists of water, protein, dextrose, ash, and traces of egg oil. In painting, it is referred to as *glair*. Once it was extensively used in painting illuminated manuscripts. When mixed with pigments, white of egg is somewhat brittle; and, as compared with gum arabic (which is a more powerful binder), its only advantage is that it becomes water-insoluble when dry.

In its natural state the white of egg is too stringy to be used as a medium. It should, therefore, first be beaten to a froth and permitted to stand, whereupon it turns to a clear liquid. An addition of a few drops of vinegar will keep it from putrefying. Pigments to be used with this binder should first be ground in water to a liquid paste, as for an egg yolk binder.

CHAPTER 19

Oil-Tempera Painting

476. *Q. What is the definition of the term "oil tempera"?*

A. Oil tempera points to the introduction of oil (or oil and resin) into the egg-water medium described in the previous chapter. This distinction is used in this book to differentiate between these two types of tempera, since the term "tempera" does not seem precise enough.

477. *Q. What are the general uses of oil tempera in painting?*

A. Oil tempera may be used for underpainting a picture that is to be finished in straight oil, or a painting may be executed entirely in oil tempera.

478. *Q. What emulsifying agent other than egg may be used for tempera painting?*

A. Gum arabic. However, egg is considered the more desirable ingredient for oil-tempera emulsions because of its excellent drying properties, the toughness and elasticity of its film, and its balanced properties as an emulsifier. Moreover, egg becomes water-insoluble in time. Gum arabic-oil emulsion produces a paint which remains hygroscopic and dries very slowly.

479. *Q. What is an emulsion and what types of emulsion may be used?*

A. We have already seen (Q. 448) that an emulsion is a suspension of one liquid in another. When two non-miscible liquids, such as oil and water, are emulsified, the nature of the suspension may vary in several ways. First, oil drops may be suspended in water; second, water drops can be suspended in oil; and third, there can be a multiple suspension in which the smaller globules of the dispersed liquid contain still smaller drops within them. The first type of suspension takes place when the colloidal egg-water-oil solution is emulsified with linseed oil, and the second is formed when the stabilizer is water-insoluble—that is, when it is a colloidal solution in oil rather than in an aqueous liquid. This seems to be the case when a resin acts as a stabilizer. A multiple suspension apparently takes place when both stabilizers are present—the one with water affinity (egg) and the other with oil affinity (resin). The quantitative relation of water and oil is not responsible for forming either kind of emulsion. Water-in-oil emulsion may be thinned with oil only. For example: egg yolk, 1 part; standoil, 1 part (this may be diluted with some turpentine). Oil-in-water emulsion may be thinned with water, for example: egg, 2 parts; water, 3 parts; standoil, 1 part.

480. *Q. What are the conditions for keeping a stable emulsion?*

A. In order to remain in suspension, the drops of the liquid must be sufficiently small and they must be surrounded with a viscous film which prevents coalescing.

481. *Q. What kind of pigments should be used for oil-tempera painting?*

A. Powdered pigments, the same as are used in oil painting.

482. *Q. Are the pigments ground in the emulsion, and does the emulsion serve as a painting medium?*

A. The emulsion is a binder for the pigments as well as the painting medium, although one may thin the paints with a thinned emulsion or with water.

483. *Q. What are the common emulsion formulas?*

A. Besides the formulas mentioned in the answer to Question 479, the most frequently used is: whole egg, 1 part; standoil, ½ to 1 part; damar varnish (heavy solution), ½ to 1 part; water, 2 parts.

484. *Q. How should one prepare an emulsion?*

A. Beat one whole egg to a froth and mix it with standoil; add the damar varnish and, lastly, water. Add the water drop by drop, continuously stirring until it is perfectly emulsified with the other ingredients. Twenty drops of vinegar added to 1 pint of the emulsion will serve as a preservative. When stored in a well-stopped bottle in a cool place, it will remain in a fresh condition for weeks or even months.

485. *Q. Should one prepare the tempera paints or buy them in tubes?*

A. It is considered better practice to prepare one's own paints. However, some of the commercial paints are reliable—that is, they may be looked upon as permanent when they stand the following test, as devised by A. P. Laurie: A quantity of tube paint should be mixed with water and painted on a glass slide; also a lump of paint as it comes from the tube should be squeezed onto a glass slide. After a month the paint should solidify without cracking. The glass slide should then be submerged in hot (not boiling) water and left in it for several hours. At the end of that time, neither the film of paint nor the lump of paint should have dissolved or become detached from the glass.

486. *Q. How should one grind tempera colors, and in what way does the procedure differ from grinding oil colors?*

A. Oil paints are ground to a soft consistency with a muller, under considerable pressure, each with a definite amount of oil. In the case of tempera, mixing of pigments with the emulsion by means of a stiff palette knife to a loose consistency is sufficient. Storage of oil-tempera paint is impractical.

487. *Q. What type of palette should be used, and how can one keep these colors from drying on the palette?*

A. The palette may be made of glass, metal, or plastic, and may be equipped with cups. Glass tumblers (inverted) can then be employed to cover up the paint.

488. *Q. What type of support should be used for oil-tempera painting?*

A. Because oil-tempera paints do not have the elasticity of straight oil paints, a rigid support is preferable to canvas. A semiabsorbent gesso (glue or casein) is more suitable than an oil ground. Tempera painting will not adhere well to a nonabsorbent ground.

489. *Q. Should one apply the paints thinly or with impasto?*

A. A well-prepared tempera paint will not crack no matter how strong its impasto—providing that it is applied to a rigid support.

490. *Q. What are the advantages of oil-tempera underpainting?*

A. Recently carried out microchemical analyses of van Eyck's paintings have shown that, contrary to the hitherto accepted belief, the underpainting was done in straight oil paint, not in tempera. Hence it became evident that underpainting in tempera offers no particular advantage.

491. *Q. How can an application of oil tempera be overpainted by another layer of oil tempera and then by straight resin-oil paint?*

A. Depending on the thickness of the paint film, tempera overpainting may be carried out in a few days or longer. Oil painting can follow as soon as the underpainting solidifies.

492. *Q. Should one use retouching varnish between the layers of oil-tempera paint?*

A. Not necessarily, though the adhesion of the paint film will always be improved in presence of varnish.

493. *Q. How should one finish a painting in straight oil tempera?*

A. When painting in straight oil tempera is planned, it is advisable to increase the oil content of the emulsion in the top paint layers. However, too much oil will make the paint behave just as in straight oil painting.

494. *Q. How are oil glazes applied on top of oil-tempera underpaintings?*

A. Depending on the nature of the paint stratum, a week or more after its completion a tempera underpainting should be covered with copal varnish in order to make the underpainting less absorbent, hence better adapted to the application of glazes. One may paint on a rough underpainting, or one may smooth down an impasto with fine sandpaper or steel wool.

495. *Q. Should an oil-tempera painting be varnished?*

A. Varnishing in the same manner as in oil painting is recommended. (For varnishing, *see* Q. 181-193.)

496. *Q. What are other characteristics of oil-tempera painting?*

A. Tempera painting is short and more crisp; viscosity of the medium is very low, hence the structure of the brush-stroke is sharp, and particularly suitable for executing draftsmanlike effects.

497. *Q. How does the permanence of the oil-tempera paint compare with that of straight oil paint?*

A. In time, tempera paint solidifies to a film that is harder and more impervious to the action of moisture, gases, and volatile solvents than the film of oil paint.

498. *Q. Is it necessary to varnish tempera paintings?*

A. Because of the particular quality of its surface a tempera painting can remain unvarnished for a long time.

499. *Q. Should a tempera painting be waxed?*

A. A wax-varnish is best for the purpose. Since tempera is executed on a rigid support, waxing is therefore most appropriate.

500. *Q. What are the shortcomings of tempera painting?*

A. It does not allow blending of colors in the manner of oil painting. Hence its texture is less sensuous and its general appearance rather dry.

INDEX*

Academy board, 19, 20
Acetone, 39, 41, 42
Acidity of oil, 34-35
Adhesives, 28-31; see also Casein; Gelatin; Glue; Gum arabic
Alcohol, 39, 41, 42, 61
Alizarin crimson, 71-72, 75
"Alla prima" painting, 107
Aluminum hydrate, 60, 75
Aluminum stearate, 59, 63, 77, 78, 79, 80
Ammonia, 39, 41
Anhydrous alcohol, 41
Atomizer, use for varnishing, 52-53
Azurite blue, 95-96

Balsams, 54-55
Barium yellow, 72
Barytes, 89
Beeswax, 52, 57, 78-79, 80, 120
Benzene, 39, 41, 42
Benzol, 41
Binder, 10
Black colors, 75, 94, 106
Bleaching, yellowed ground, 10
Bloom, 54; causes and remedy, 117; defined, 117
Blown oil, defined, 37
Blow-pipe test, 88-89, 90
Blue colors, 70-71; difference between, 70; old masters' pigments, 95-96; testing, 89; tints, 113; use, 70-71
Bone black, 93-94
Brazil wood, 94
Bristle brushes, 24
Brown colors, 74
Brushes, 24-26; bristle, 24; cleaning, 26; dried paint from, removing, 26; egg-tempera painting, 130; gessoing, 25; glazing with, 111; kinds, 24; lengthening, 25-26; reshaping, 26; resin from, removing, 26; sable, 24; soft-hair blender, 25; trimming, 25; underpainting with, 104; varnishing, 25, 52
Bulges on canvas, flattening, 117, 118

Burnt sienna, 71-72

Cadmium, barium paints, 73; colors, testing, 90; orange, 73; red, 71-72; sulphide, 73; yellow, 72-73
Calcium carbonate, 88
Canvas, 9-12; casein priming on, 22; choosing, 9-10; cotton, 9; damaged, repairing, 119; ground, 10; ironing, 122; linen, 9; most commonly used, 9; preparing, 11; priming, 12-15; sandpapering, 12; sizing, 11-12
Caput mortuum, 65, 66, 79, 92
Carnauba wax, 58
Casein, 28, 30-31; advantages for gessoing, 22; decomposition, preventing, 22-23; defined, 22, 30-31; latex cement, 121; preservatives, 60-61; priming with, 22-23, solution, preparing, 22
Ceresin, 58
Cerulean blue, 70; use, 71
China clay, 59-60
China wood oil, 38
Chrome oxide green, opaque, 74; testing, 89
Clay, 59-60, 79, 80, 89
Cleaning, brushes, 26; paintings, 42, 53, 114-17
Cobalt, 43; blue, 70, 71; linoleate, 43; naphthanate, 43
Cochineal, 94
Colophony, 39
Colors, selecting, 75-76; see also Pigments
Composition board, 17-18; defined 17; kinds, 17; oil priming, 23; priming 20; reinforced, 17-18; thickness, 18
Congo copal, 45, 46-47
Consistency, paint, 80-81
Copaiba balsam, 55
Copal, 45, 46-47, 48, 50, 110-11
Copal Concentrate, 50, 56, 68, 83
Copal Painting Medium, 13, 56, 103, 104, 106
Cottonseed oil, 38
Cracked areas, 118

Reference numbers indicate pages.

139

Cracking, 123-24
Cradling, 19
Creases on canvas, smoothing, 117, 118

Damar, 45-46, 47, 49, 110-11
Dirt, removing from painting, 114, 115
Dowcide, 61
Drawing, transfer of, 101
Dryers, see Siccatives
Dry paint, palette knife used for scraping, 27; preventing, 85; removing from brush, 26
Dust, removing, 114

Earth colors, 64-65; body of, 64-65; composition, 64; drying capacity, 64; mars colors compared with, 65; old masters' pigments, 92; opacity of, 64-65; permanency, 64; quality, testing, 89-90; tinting capacity, 65
Egg-tempera painting, 127-32
Egg-white, use, 131-32
Egg yoke, properties, 127
Emulsions, egg-tempera painting, 127; oil-tempera painting, 133-34, 135

Fish oil, 38
Fixative, 41
Flake white, see White lead
Flesh tints, 113
Flour paste, 120
Free acid in oil, 34-35

Gelatin, 28, 30; advantages, 30; decomposition, preventing, 30; defined 30; kinds, 30; used as size, 11
Gesso ground, 14-15; absorbency, 21-22; application, 15, 21; brushes for, 25; decomposition, prevention, 15; defined, 14; painting on, 21; priming with, 14, 20-22; strong or weak glue content, 15; titanium white, use, 20; use, 14-15
Glazing, 109-12; application, 111; cleaning, 114-15; colors used for, 110; defined, 109; execution, 111; hue of underpainting and, 112; medium best for, 110; oil-tempera painting, 137; overpainting,

111-12; permanency, 112; resin most suitable for, 110-11; technique development, 110; time for, 111; types of, 111
Glue, 28-29, 120; best quality, 28; characteristics of good, 28; decomposition, preventing, 29; dissolving, 29; kinds to avoid, 29; made from, 28; preservatives, 60-61; recognizing good, 29; used as size, 11
Gray tints, 113
Green colors, 74; testing, 89; tints, 113
Green earth pigment, 60, 79, 80, 92
Grinding oil, 82-83
Grinding pigments by hand, 77-85; grinding oil, 82-83; paint consistency, 80-81; pigments, 83-85; stabilizers, 78-80; studio-prepared paint, advantage, 77; tools, 81-81
Grisaille, 105-06; advantages, 105: colors used for, 105-06; defined, 105; old masters' use of, 106
Ground, 10-11; bleaching, 10; gesso, 14-15; gray, 10; oil, 12-14; studio-prepared, 11; toned, 103; type, 10; white lead, 10; yellowing, 10
Gum arabic, 28, 31
Gums, 45, 60-61
Gypsum, 93

Hansa yellow, 72, 73, 75
Holes, repairing, 119

Illustration board, 17, 19; permanency, 20; sizing, 19-20
Imprimatura, 101-03; application, 102; colors used for, 102; defined, 101-02; drying time, 102-03: purpose, 101-02; thinning medium used for, 102; used on top of underpainting, 104; when to use, 102
Indian, red, 71-72; yellow, 95
Indigo, 96
Ironing the canvas, 122
Iron oxides, 79
Ivory black, 75

Kaolin, 59
Kerosene, 39, 41

Labeling of commercial tube paints, 86-87
Lake colors, 75
Lamp black, 93, 94
Lapis lazuli, 95
Laurie, A. P., 135
"Leveling" of oil, 33-34
Light fastness, testing paint for, 91
Linen canvas, 9
Linoxyn, 33
Linseed oil, 32-37; advantages, 33; blown oil, 37; cold-pressed, defined, 32; disadvantages, 33; exposure to sun, 36; free acid in, 34-35; industrial, 33; leveling of, 33-34; neutral, characteristics, 34; polymerization, 35-36; refining, 32-33; stand-oil, 33, 36-37; sun-thickened, 35-36; thinning, solvents for, 42; wetting power, 33; yellowing causes, 33
Lint, removing, 114
"Long" paint, defined, 34, 35

Madder lake, 75, 94
Malachite, 95
Manganese, 43; blue, 70, 71, 89
Mars colors, 65-66, 79; black, 66, 75; brown, 74; caput mortuum and mars violet, difference between, 66; colors used in painting, 66; defined, 65; earth colors compared with, 65; violet, 65, 66, 71-72
Masonite, see Composition board
Massicot, 93
Mastic, 42, 45-46, 47
Methyl alcohol, 41, 61
Mineral spirits, 39, 40, 42
Minium, 93, 94
Modern colors, how old are, 97
Monastral colors, 70, 74, 75
Muller, 81, 84

Naphtha, 41
Naples yellow, 72, 93

Oil ground, 12-14
Oil of cloves, 38
Oil paints, adulteration, 87-88, 89; black colors, 75; blue colors; 70-71; brown colors, 74; casein priming for, 22; cheap vs. expensive, 62; colors inclined to yellow, 64; consistency, 80-81; earth colors, 64-65; European-made vs. domestic, 61-62; green colors, 74; hardening in tubes, 63; lake colors, 75; limpid in tubes, 63; mars colors, 65-66; palette knife used with, 27; pigments and, 61-76; popular colors to avoid, 62-63; red colors, 71-72; reducing to dry pigment, 91; selecting colors, 75-76; storing, 85; tests of, 86-91; thin, improving, 64; time usable when kept in tube, 63-64; tint as indicator of quality, 62; tinting of a color, testing, 62; white colors, 66-70; yellow colors, 72-73
Oil priming, 23
Oils, 32-38; see also Grinding oil; Linseed oil; Poppy-seed oil; Walnut oil
Oil-tempera painting, 133-38
Old masters, grisaille used by, 106; pigments, 92-97; wood panels used by, 18, 19
Oleo-resins, see Balsams
Overpainting, 107, 108-09; cracked area, 118; egg-tempera painting, 130; glaze with opaque color, 111-12; number of layers, 108-09; oil-tempera painting, 136-37; trickling of, 108
Ozokerite, 58

Painting, 107-09; "alla prima," 107; color contrast with underpainting, 109; flat paint surface, 108; glossy paint surface, 107-08; layer on top of another, applying, 108; overpainting, see Overpainting; paint film, removing, 109; resinous medium, use of, 107; starting with dark or light values, 109; tempera, see Egg-tempera, Oil-tempera; trickling of overpainting, 108; underpainting, see Underpainting
Painting medium formulas, 55-57
Paint removers, commercial, 42

Palette, painter's color arrangement on 76; colors for beginners' 75-76; kinds, 27; oil-tempera painting, 136

Palette knife, filling holes with, 119; glazing with, 111; grinding pigments with, 84; priming with, 14; sizing with, 12; toned ground applied with, 103; types and uses, 27; underpainting with, 104

Panels, 9, 16-23; advantages, 16; canvas 9-15; disadvantages, 16; gesso ground on, 15; wood, see Wood panels

Paraffin, 42; wax, 58

Patch, applying, 120

Permanency, egg-tempera painting, 131; glazing, 112; illustration board, 20; oil paintings, conditions detrimental to, 122-23; oil-tempera painting, 138

Phenol, 61

Phthalocyanine blue, 70, 74

Pigments, black colors, 75; blue colors, 70-71; brown colors, 74; defined, 61; domestic and imported, 62; earth colors, 64-65; egg medium combined with, 128; green colors, 74; grinding, 83-85; lake colors, 75; mars colors, 65-66; old masters', 92-97; oil paints and, 61-76; oil-tempera painting, 134; palette knife for mixing, 27; red colors, 71-72; reducing oil paint to, 91; studio tube, amount needed to fill, 84; tests of, 86-91; white colors, 66-70; yellow colors, 72-73

Pink tints, 113

Plate glass, ground, 81

Plywood, 17; advantages, 18; best obtainable, 18; defined, 18; durability, increasing, 20

Polymerized oil, 35-36

Poppy-seed oil, 32, 37-38

Preservatives, 60-61

Priming, 12-15; application, 14; casein, 22-23; drying, 14; egg-tempera painting, 129; gesso ground, 14-15; 20-22; layers applied 13-14; Masonite panel, 20; oil ground, 12-14, 23; painting on, 14; time between, 14; white lead for, 13

Prussian blue, 70; testing, 89; use 70-71

Putty, 119; knife, 27

Red colors, 71-72; differences between, 71; old masters' pigments, 94-95; tints, 113; use, 71-72

Relining, procedure in, 121-22; support for, 120

Resins, 42, 45-49; adhesive, using, 122; cleaning from brush, 26; commonly used, 46; cracking and discoloration caused by, 48; defined, 45; dissolving, 47; soft and hard, 45-46; solvent for cutting, 41-42; sources, 45; synthetic, 54

Restoring, 117-24

Rome, ancient, colors used in, 97

Rosin, defined, 39

Sable brushes, 24

Sandpapering, gesso ground, 21

Saponification of white lead, 67

Saponine, 42

Scratches, filling, 118

Scumbling, 112-13; colors useful for, 112; defined, 112; execution, 112; permanency, 112-13

"Short" paint, defined, 34

Siccatif de Courtrai, 44

Siccatif de Haarlem, 44

Siccatives, 43-44; safest, 43; use in underpainting, 105

Sinopia, 92

Size and sizing, 11-12; applying, 11; back of canvas, 12; formula, 11; illustration board, 19-20; liquid or gelled, 11-12; purpose, 11; putrefying, prevention, 12; strong or weak, 12

Smalt, 96

Soap and water cleaning with, 116

Solvents, 39-42, 114-15

Soya bean oil, 38

Stabilizers, 78-80

Standoil, 33, 36-37; 82; characteristics, 36-37; defined, 36; uniformity, 37

Sun-thickened oil, 35-36

Supports,, 9-12; 129; **see also** Canvas; Composition boards; Illustration board; Panels; Plywood; Wood panels

Tears in canvas, repairing, 119
Tempera painting, **see** Egg-Tempera painting; Oil-tempera painting,
Terra di pozzuoli, 92
Tests, paints and pigments, 86-91; blow-pipe test, 88-89; colors, various, 89-91; light fastness, 91; organic dye, for presence of, 88
Tints, various, 113
Titanium white, 68-69; composition, 68-69; hiding power, 20; merits of, 69; reliability, 68-69; tones when mixed with other colors, 69; white lead superior to, 69
Toluene, 41
Toned ground, 103
Tools, grinding, 81-82
Transfer of drawing, 101
Trickling, of overpainting, 108; varnish, preventing, 53
Tung oil, 38
Turpentine, 39-40, 42; derivation, 39; recognizing good, 40; rosin in, 39; steam-distilled, 40; storage, 40; trade names for best, 39

Ultramarine blue, 70; testing, 89; use, 71
Umber, 44, 74, 92
Underpainting, 104-06; color contrast with, painting in, 109; colors used in, 104; defined, 104; drying time, 104-05; egg-tempera painting, 130; grisaille, 105-06; historical use of, 105; imprimatura used on, 104; oiling, 106; oil-tempera painting, 136; painting medium used in, 104; palette knife used for, 27; siccative in, 105; tools used for, 104; value of, 104; zinc white used for, 70

Varnishes and varnishing, 45-54; application, 51-52; atomizer for, use, 52-53; brittle and fissured film, 53-54; brushes for, 25, 52; commercial, 48-49; copal, uses, 50; damar, 49; defined, 45; deterioration, 50; drying time, 50; durability, 53; egg-tempera painting, 130-31; in oil medium, 55-56; mat, 52; moisture, removing before, 54; oil-tempera painting, 137, 138; on humid days, 54; removing from fresh painting, 114; retouching, purposes, 49, 51; synthetic resin, 54; trickling of, 53
Venetian red, 71-72
Verdigris, 95
Verditer, 96
Vermilion, 71-72, 94; testing, 91
Vine black, 94
Violet tints, 113
Veridian green, 74; testing, 89

Wallpaper paste, 120
Walnut oil, 32, 38
Waxes, 49, 57-58; egg-tempera painting, 131; oil-tempera painting, 138; using, procedure, 122
"Wetting power" of oil, 33
White colors, 55-70; titanium white, 68-69; white lead, 66-68; zinc white, 69-70
White lead, 66-68; adulterants of, 89; affect on other colors, 66; canned, use in painting, 13, 68; gessoing with, 21; ground, 10; old masters' pigments, 93; poisonousness, 67; priming with, 13; reaction with oil of high acid value, 68; reaction with polymerized oil, 68; saponification of, 67; "short" to "long," changing, 68; superior pigment, 67, 69; tempera white mixed with, 68; yellowing of, 66-67
Whiting, 88, 89
Wood, 96
Wood panels, 17; disadvantages, 19: kinds used by old masters, 18, 19; warping, prevention, 19

Xylene, 39, 41, 42

Yellow colors, 72-73; differences between, 72; old masters' pigments, 95; tints, 113; use, 72-73

Zanzibar copal, 46

Zinc yellow, 72-73; testing, 90

Zinc white, 69-70; adulterants of, 89; influence on other colors, 70; underpainting with, 70; use of, 69